20.00

Inscribed by compiler

Cover spotted

THE DANCE PHOTOGRAPHY OF CARL VAN VECHTEN

Mill Valley
Dec 12, 1981

Dear Bill -

It is a great pleasure to inscribe this copy of Carl's photographs for you. I am grateful for your encouragement in my CVV writing projects; may you enjoy the results of this labour of love.

With affection
Paul

Martha Graham and Bertram Ross in *Clytemnestra*, 1961

THE DANCE
PHOTOGRAPHY
OF
CARL VAN VECHTEN

SELECTED
AND WITH AN INTRODUCTION BY
PAUL PADGETTE

SCHIRMER BOOKS
A Division of Macmillan Publishing Co., Inc.
New York
Collier Macmillan Publishers
London

SCHIRMER BOOKS
A Division of Macmillan Publishing Co., Inc.
866 Third Avenue, New York, N.Y. 10022

Collier Macmillan Canada, Ltd.

Library of Congress Catalog Card Number: 81-51117

Printed in the United States of America

printing number
1   2   3   4   5   6   7   8   9   10

Library of Congress Cataloging in Publication Data

Van Vechten, Carl, 1880–1964.
   The dance photography of Carl Van Vechten.

   Bibliography: p.
   1. Dance—Pictorial works. I. Padgette,
Paul. II. Title.
GV1596.V36 1981   793.3   81-51117
ISBN 0-02-872680-4   AACR2

Dedicated to the Memory
of
Carl Van Vechten
(1880–1964)

ACKNOWLEDGMENTS

My first acknowledgement must be to my editor at Dance Horizons, Al Pischl, who suggested I embark on this venture to bring Carl Van Vechten's dance photography to a larger public. I thank Donald Gallup, Van Vechten's literary trustee and Curator of American Literature, Beinecke Rare Book and Manuscript Library, Yale University, for his encouragement and suggestions after reading an early draft of the Introduction, and for granting permission to extract passages from the unpublished Van Vechten Columbia Oral Interview and from Van Vechten letters to several correspondents. Mr. Gallup kindly authorized the prints made from the original Van Vechten negatives of photographs in the Yale Library. I welcomed the opportunity of meeting Joseph Solomon, who represents the Van Vechten Estate, and I thank him for his permission to publish the photographs in this book. Carl Van Vechten's photographs may not be reproduced without written permission of the Estate of Carl Van Vechten. I wish to thank Martha Swope for her permission to publish her copyrighted photograph of Martha Graham and Carl Van Vechten.

My task was made easier by the cooperation of a number of people: Michael Nash, Annex Archivist, New York Public Library; Henry Wisnecki and Wennie Messe, Dance Collection, Performing Arts Research Center, Lincoln Center, New York; Aldo R. Cupo and Karen Marinuzzi, Yale University Library.

Sincere thanks are due to the artist George George, for granting me a stimulating interview in October 1979 in New York City, and for allowing me to use quotations from letters to him from Carl Van Vechten. I owe a large debt of appreciation to Bruce Kellner, Van Vechten's biographer and bibliographer, for allowing me to quote from his biography, *Carl Van Vechten and the Irreverent Decades*, and to excerpt passages from his letters from Van Vechten. Most of all I value his continuing interest in this project and his careful reading of the manuscript. Again, I sincerely thank and owe a debt of gratitude to Desmond Arthur, my mentor and severest critic, for his patient assistance during the preparation of this book.

Paul Padgette

SOURCES

Barnes, Clive. Introduction and commentaries. In *Inside American Ballet Theatre*. New York: Hawthorn, 1977.

Calloway, Cab, and Bryant Rollins. *Of Minnie the Moocher and Me*. New York: Crowell, 1976.

Chujoy, Anatole. *The New York City Ballet*. New York: Knopf, 1953.

Chujoy, Anatole, and P.W. Manchester, compilers and editors. *The Dance Encyclopedia*, revised and enlarged edition. New York: Simon and Schuster, 1967.

de Mille, Agnes. *Dance to the Piper*. Boston: Little, Brown, 1952.

de Mille, Agnes. *The Book of the Dance*. New York: Golden Press, 1963.

Denby, Edwin. *Looking at the Dance*. New York: Pellegrini & Cudahy, 1949.

Ewen, David. *A Journey to Greatness: The Life and Music of George Gershwin*. New York: Holt, 1956.

Gruen, John. *The Private World of Ballet*. New York: Viking, 1975.

Haskins, Jim. *The Cotton Club*. New York: Random House, 1977.

Hughes, Langston, and Milton Meltzer. *Black Magic: A Pictorial History of Black Entertainers in America*. Englewood Cliffs, N.J.: Prentice-Hall, 1967.

Isaacs, Edith J. R. *The Negro in the American Theatre*. New York: Theatre Arts, 1947.

Kellner, Bruce. *Carl Van Vechten and the Irreverent Decades*. Norman: University of Oklahoma Press, 1968.

Krokover, Rosalyn. *The New Borzoi Book of Ballets*. New York: Knopf, 1956.

Lueders, Edward. *Carl Van Vechten*. New York: Twayne, 1965.

Markova, Alicia. *Giselle and I*. London: Barrie And Rockliff, 1960.

McDonagh, Don. *The Rise and Fall and Rise of Modern Dance*. New York: Outerbridge & Dienstfrey, 1970.

McDonagh, Don. *Martha Graham*. New York: Praeger, 1973.

Padgette, Paul. *Carl Van Vechten*. San Francisco: Bindweed Press, 1965.

Padgette, Paul. *The Dance Writings of Carl Van Vechten*. New York: Dance Horizons, 1974.

Reynolds, Nancy, editor. *The Dance Catalog*. New York: Harmony Books, 1979.

Robert, Grace. *The Borzoi Book of Ballets*. New York: Knopf, 1946.

Taper, Bernard. *Balanchine*. New York: Harper & Row, 1963.

Terry, Walter. *Star Performance: The Story of the World's Great Ballerinas*. Garden City, N.Y.: Doubleday, 1954.

Terry, Walter. *The Dance in America*, revised edition. New York: Harper & Row, 1971.

Barrett, John Townsend. "Analysis and Significance of Three American Critics of the Ballet: Carl Van Vechten, Edwin Denby, and Lincoln Kirstein." M.F.A. thesis, Columbia University, 1955.

"The Reminiscences of Carl Van Vechten: A Rudimentary Narration." Typescript of interviews tape-recorded by William Ingersoll for the Oral History Research Office of Columbia University, New York, 1960.

Dance Magazine, January 1980

Dance Index, Volume 1, Nos. 9,10,11, September-October-November 1942

Esquire, December 1962

New York Globe, 1915-1916

New York Public Library Bulletin, July 1955; October-December 1966

New York State Theatre *Program*, January 1965

New York Times, 1910-1912

The Reviewer, Richmond, Virginia, July 1922

Theatre Arts, December 1942; October 1943; November 1951

Village Voice, New York, September 27, 1962

Yale University Library Gazette, April 1965

INTRODUCTION

Carl Van Vechten's career as a photographer was the third and most fervent one he enjoyed in a long, productive life. Between 1932 and 1964, when he died, he produced thousands of photographs that are different from any others created in this century.

Born in 1880 in Cedar Rapids, Iowa, he was graduated from the University of Chicago in 1903, and worked as a reporter on that city's newspapers for three years. In 1906 he moved to New York and became assistant music critic under Richard Aldrich at the *New York Times*, and in 1908–1909 represented that paper as its Paris correspondent. Aldrich, a typical music critic of the day, preferred traditional nineteenth-century music and sent his assistant to review performances of newer compositions. It was in this way that Van Vechten began to see dance programs, which were often staged at the end of an evening of opera. More excited by these than by the routine opera performances, he wrote enthusiastically about them, thus becoming the first reviewer to write in the daily press about dance in America. In the next few years he reported on the first major appearances in America of Isadora Duncan, Loie Fuller, and Maud Allan, American dancers who found their first fame in Europe. He was the first critic to attend and review the debuts of Pavlova and Mordkin, Nijinsky, and the initial tours of the Russian Ballet in the United States.

On February 28, 1910, the day Pavlova debuted at the Metropolitan Opera House, dancing the first two acts of *Coppélia* as an afterpiece to the opera *Werther*, Van Vechten interviewed her for the *Times*, a common practice today but not in 1910. It was the first interview Pavlova granted and his review of her debut in the *Times* the next day was the first to appear in America.

In his interview he quotes Mlle. Pavlova detailing the popularity of ballet in St. Petersburg: "The ballet is as important at the Imperial Opera as the production of opera itself. Two nights a week the ballet is given, and the other nights opera. These ballets are long. They last from 8 o'clock until 12. Not a word is sung—it is all pantomime and dancing—and there is as great a subscription for these nights as there is for the opera." She was asked her opinion of Isadora Duncan: "I have seen Miss Duncan and I admire her dancing. What difference does it make what sort of dancing one does? . . . One has to be adept in the art, to know it from its foundations, and all about it." When asked her opinion of New York she gave the standard tourist reply: "I am fascinated with the city. All of it is so tall! But will it be fascinated with me?"

As we know, it was. A few days later the Pavlova-Mordkin company moved to the New Theatre to continue performances of *Coppélia* (the first act only), this time following an evening of *Madama Butterfly*. In his review on March 5, 1910, Van Vechten tells us that the house was sold out for the first time in its existence, "at least on an opera night." He ends his enthusiastic review by suggesting, "Why not give the entire ballet with a one-act opera?" Pavlova was so much a success she and Mordkin returned in the fall of 1910 for a five-month season, and after two extended periods during the winter at the Metropolitan Opera House toured to the West Coast and to Cuba.

The popular Pavlova-Mordkin company toured regularly for several seasons. Other "Russian" companies, such as the one featuring Gertrude Hoffmann, made their own tours, dancing in the major cities in competition. Ballet in America was Russian ballet. This was an accepted fact with American theatregoing audiences until the 1930s and 1940s, when Ballet Theatre and other American dance companies showed the public that ballet was international and included American themes as well.

In the *New York Globe* for February 11, 1915, appeared a review of the first American appearance of the Spanish dancer, La Argentina, at the Maxine Elliott Theatre. Van Vechten was strong in his praise for the dancer. It is interesting that *The Dance Encyclopedia* (revised edition, 1967) dates this performance a year later, in January 1916, and reports that it was sparsely attended and not covered by any critic. In his review Van Vechten says it was performed before "an audience which included such distinguished personalities as Lucrezia Bori, Yvette Guilbert, Josef Hofman, Ernest Schelling, and Enrico Granados. . . . With infinite skill and unflagging virtuosity the dancer gives examples of the various dances which her country is so prolific in producing. Several times her naïveté of expression stood her in good stead, for Spanish dancing is not dancing for prudes. Her sense of rhythm was truly remarkable, and some of her most subtle effects were made with the slight tap of a heel, the bend of a knee on the beat, or the quiver of an eyelash to accompany a trill of the flute. . . ." It was a number of years before the famous dancer was able to play to large audiences in America. Spanish dance had not yet arrived as popular theatre, although Van Vechten was doing his best to develop an audience for it.

In November 1917 (*The Dance Encyclopedia* in error says 1919) La Argentina appeared in New York again, at the Park Theatre in *The Land of Joy*, a program composed by Joaquin Valverde, in which she shared billing with Doloretes and a cast including Spanish singers. Van Vechten's long review, splattered with superlatives, ended, "I walked out into Columbus Circle completely purged of pity and fear, love, hate, and all the rest. It was an experience."

Ever campaigning for the new and novel in music, Van Vechten in January 1915 wrote in the *New York Globe*: "In certain instances, notably in Stravinsky's *Firebird* and *Petrouchka*, New Yorkers were introduced to the most interesting modern music by perhaps the greatest of the young composers." Fifty-five years later, in 1970, dance critic Don McDonagh noted that Van Vechten "had an enormous sympathy for dance and wrote some of the most perceptive criticism on dance that the country has ever seen."

In 1920, at the age of forty, Van Vechten gave up day-to-day music and dance reviewing. During the previous fifteen years he had also worked as a drama reviewer (in 1913-1914 for the *New York Post*), authored program notes for the New York Symphony Society, and had seen seven volumes of his criticism through publication. He felt as he arrived at forty that he was no longer able to judge music, dance, and drama in an objective way, that "the cells hardened and that prejudices were formed which precluded the possibility of the welcoming of novelty." He continued to pen occasional essays and introductions to books, and wrote reviews of books concerning all the arts. If the stimulus was present in sufficient amounts, Van Vechten's critical juices would flow again, helping the creative efforts of young persons he admired and wished to assist.

His first project after retiring from criticism was to compile and publish a thick volume concerning all aspects of feline culture. *Tiger in the House* (1920), still the essential study of the cat, went through five editions and remained in print for over half a century.

In 1922 he collected a number of autobiographical fragments, some of which had been published separately in wide-ranging journals, and expanded them into a novel, *Peter Whiffle, His Life and Works*. In the book, he appears as himself, while a part of himself appears as Peter Whiffle. Many famous people in the arts on both sides of the Atlantic whom he had met during his years as a critic make appearances, either named outright or thinly veiled as fictional characters. The novel was an immediate best seller and went through twelve printings. In 1927 an illustrated, revised edition was published; the Modern Library issued an edition in 1929.

Van Vechten wrote seven novels that were popular with readers and critics. In 1930 he published his last, *Parties*, which was called by one critic "a novel about the death of the twenties." The distinguishing feature in all his novels is a carefully chiseled comedy of manners style, even when his subject is a serious one, as in *Nigger Heaven* (1926). This novel about Harlem aroused the wrath of some members of black society as well as that of certain white critics. The title was found offensive and many who condemned it admitted to not having read it. The novel went through nine printings in the first four months after publication and subsequently appeared in ten foreign-language editions. In recent years it has been reissued in two different paper editions. To a later generation *Nigger Heaven* is creative and imaginative, and a phenomenal work to be published by a white author in the twenties.

In a memoir, *Sacred and Profane Memories* (1932), Van Vechten remembered that photography had held a fascination for him even in his teens when, using a clumsy box camera, he snapped a fine Whistler's Mother mood-photo of his grandmother in Iowa. There are extant several interesting mid-distance photographs taken early in this century of Luisa Tetrazzini emerging from the *Times* building in New York and Olive Fremstad and Charles Dalmores in the Luxembourg Gardens in Paris. By the time he took the latter he was using a Kodak.

In the early 1930s the artist Miguel Covarrubias returned from Europe with a Leica camera. He was enthusiastic in his praise of the new German invention and showed Van Vechten some of his experiments with it. It was an opportune time, as Van Vechten had recently completed what was to be his last book, and a new project intrigued him. He immediately purchased a Leica and began his own experiments. The earliest subjects were his wife, Fania Marinoff, an actress and a superb subject whom he photographed hundreds of times over the years, and friends from the twenty-five years of associations in the arts in New York. Many self-portraits* date from this early period in his new profession. (Asterisks throughout this Introduction indicate subjects whose photographs are included in the book.) Van Vechten had begun the third and most passionate of his careers in the arts.

Among his early sitters were the Chinese actress Anna May Wong, playwright Eugene O'Neill and his actress wife Carlotta Monterey (he made dozens of portrait studies of them), Tallulah Bankhead, H. L. Mencken, Helen Morgan, and Paul Muni. Bill "Bojangles" Robinson,* the black tap dancer and a legend in the history of the American musical theatre, was the first dancer he photo-

Carl Van Vechten, a self-portrait, February 1932

Bill "Bojangles" Robinson and Carl Van Vechten, 1941

graphed, in 1933. "Bojangles" was photographed again in 1941 in a familiar set of images exhibiting his famous impish grin, with his bowler hat balanced in his hand. Another early subject was the young dancing and singing orchestra leader from Harlem's Cotton Club, Cab Calloway,* photographed in June 1933. A nod to the past was a fragile, sensuous portrait of Orchidée (Lucille Hoff),* who had danced with Loie Fuller.

The catalog of his photographic subjects began with the big names in the arts of the era. These famous performers sat for portraits or recreated in his studio scenes in costume of specific roles. The entries in his photographic logbook grew to include lesser-known performers, who sat for Van Vechten for the first time before they were above the bottom rung of the ladder. If a sitter continued to interest him aesthetically, he would document each new role with his camera.

The first modern dance pioneer he photographed was Charles Weidman,* who in the early 1920s had been a pupil of the Denishawn company at the same time as Doris Humphrey and Martha Graham. In 1928 he founded with Humphrey a school of modern dance that lasted nearly twenty years. As a dancer and choreographer, Weidman had a great talent for creating comedy and character roles. In December 1933 Van Vechten employed a most interesting use of backgrounds in his photographs of Weidman in *School for Husbands*.

His work with photography, which began as a diversion from writing, was by now an excellent substitute. He was beginning to view his increasingly important work with a completely serious intent. Its documentary aspects became apparent to him and he chose his subjects so as to record with his camera his version of literary and theatrical history. Although, he explained, his photographs were more often than not intended as documents, it should not follow that they could not be beautiful as well. He waited for what he called the "exact second" when making photographs, and his timing was acute. From the beginning he never approved of retouching his portraits and did not allow cropping of the images, even by himself. He said, "When I make a photograph I see it as a composition."

Van Vechten has proclaimed himself an amateur, and by conventional standards this is true. He worked at his art for the love of it; he did not accept commissions nor did he sell his work as a photographer. He accepted money for his photographs only when they were used in book or magazine reproduction. Van Vechten's first biographer, Edward Lueders, has said: "It may be that by pointing to Carl Van Vechten as one of the most successful dilettantes in the land, it is possible to restore part of the importance and legitimacy—perhaps even the dignity—to that beleaguered term . . . a devoted amateur whose motive is likely to be honest homage to the arts because he finds in them great pleasure and fulfillment as a thinking, feeling human being."

In 1960 Van Vechten was interviewed by William T. Ingersoll for the Columbia Oral History series in a tape-recorded session called "The Reminiscences of Carl Van Vechten: A Rudimentary Narration." In this history he gives his reasons for remaining an amateur: "Except to magazines and books, I don't sell photographs, and so I can do exactly what I please. I give people what I want. Otherwise, nobody can get me to do anything I don't want to do, and I give them the pictures I like, I don't necessarily give them the ones they may like. I don't even ask them, because I don't want any photographs of mine around that I don't like and if I were paid for these I'd have to submit to some of the subject's demands. Magazines and books are different, because they ask for something definite, and I show them what I have and they select what they want, but they don't tell me what to photograph. I don't take photographs for magazines because they ask for them in advance. I don't do that."

This control makes his work appear at times to be uneven in the sense that certain persons and performances are not recorded, which to the casual observer may seem an omission. This is particularly true in the middle period of his photographic work, when he was an unofficial photographic recorder of the dancers of and works produced by Ballet Theatre during the 1940s.

Some people, for personal reasons, did not wish to sit for him; other people he did not wish to photograph. His amateur standing, of which he was proud, made this selectivity possible. In certain instances Van Vechten admitted to oversight and neglect in his documentation. It was often a case of subject and photographer not being able to meet at appropriate times and places. Bernard Shaw, for instance, was interested in sitting for him, but they met only at times and in places when the physical arrangements were impossible. Van Vechten wished to photograph Colette when he was in Paris in 1949, but she demurred, telling him sadly that her advanced age and arthritic condition made him too late. On the other hand, there was the impresario who would not sit because he did not think the photographer worthy of recording his celebrated profile, and the dancer who wanted to be photographed, but whose artistry Van Vechten did not sufficiently admire.

In the Oral History he explains his early motivations and procedures. During his first two years of serious photography, he had his prints commercially developed, but decided that the act of creation was not complete. "Since then [1934] I have never lost interest, because developing and printing are much the most fascinating part of photography, because you don't have anybody around but yourself and you have to do things in a very skillful way and depend entirely on yourself. When you're taking pictures, you depend somewhat on the subject, and if you have an assistant, which I have, he does the lighting. But developing and printing are fascinating, are far the most interesting side of photography. And without being what you call tricky—I never have photographs retouched, or never do tricks of any kind . . . like trimming down bodies, printing with distortions and what-not. I never do that. As I say, my interest in photography is purely documentary, and most of my photographs have been taken with certain purposes in view. Not at first, but gradually they were made for certain institutions and for certain purposes. I have never objected to photographs being beautiful or emotional, or some other qualities of that kind. I've never objected to that, but my immediate purpose is documentary. They can be beautiful and interesting and documentary too."

As illustration of the early photographs, he explains further: "The Flushing World's Fair [1940] was the first outdoor project that I ever went into very extensively. Color photography came in about that year, and I took a great many pictures in color. I have a very complete record of that fair. I have made records of several ballet companies and specific dances. I have taken Central Park practically every way but upside down. I have taken New York City very extensively . . . the times of day are very interesting. For instance, on the other side of the Park you get the sunset reflected in the windows, here [Central Park West] you get the sunrise. I've done quite a good deal with that idea. All photographers have something like that which they play with in their odd moments. I don't have to go out to do that or have anybody in."

In the Oral History he explains that finished and developed photographs of the same subject by two different photographers will be two separate creations. "Once in Man Ray's studio in Paris, we did a very extraordinary thing. He took pictures of me with *my* camera and I took pictures of him with *my* camera. The lights were the same. The pictures are entirely different. You would know the same person didn't take them. Photography's a very personal thing. It's magical, too. Well, isn't it magical? You think you have a person before you who has a very even face. She has shown every possible cooperation. She looks delightful. And then the photograph turns out to be a mess. And somebody comes up here whom you actually dislike to take, because she is so plain or ugly—that person often turns out to be a great beauty in a photograph. That is what is called being photogenic. . . . I used to be continually surprised by people that had very even features turning out to be very ugly in photography. It has something to do with how alive they are. Many people who have these very even features look dead in photographs, because they haven't any vitality to show. If your subject shows vitality in the photographs, you are usually on your way to success. I know that now, in a way, so that I can help people to achieve vitality . . . you can stir them up; you can annoy them. You can make them feel."

The most distinctive and identifying element in a Van Vechten photograph is often the background. By what may have been subconscious creative choice, the background may appear symbolic, or act as a subtle enhancement of the subject exposed to his camera. The variety of materials used is endless: fabrics, metallics, absurd props of feathers, ceramics, all employed to achieve an effect. Almost all his dance photography was done in the studio; the background may be a theatrical backdrop, but it is more likely to be a creation designed to set a mood for the work being documented.

In the Oral History he refers to his backgrounds in answer to a question from the interviewer concerning the differences between using color and black and white film: "I don't think it's very different. The photographs are on color film; that's all the difference. My policy has always been to use as much color as possible in the background instead of as little. In taking photographs in black and white, I consider backgrounds very seriously. . . . In background, you have to think entirely differently about color and black and white, because you have to know what will photograph in color, and how much. Color photography is a good deal of trouble, because I use most extravagant colors if I feel like it. . . . All the black and white pictures are entirely mine: I develop them and I print them, and work for days in the darkroom. But the color photography is done outside for me. All I do is photograph those."

Bruce Kellner, in his biography of Van Vechten's life, *Carl Van Vechten and the Irreverent Decades* (1968), describes a typical photographic seance: "A session in the Van Vechten studio was never the easiest thing to survive with savoir-faire. Sometimes, the background was already chosen; sometimes, one had to be dragged out of the catalogued rolls of materials and papers stacked on shelves against one wall of the studio. Another wall bore a fantastic collection of posters, paintings, and sketches; gimcracks and gewgaws perched on every available ledge or edge. A third wall, heavily hung with two or three sets of draperies, contained a casement window through which the subject might see, while waiting for the lenses to be focused, a lovely view of Central Park, just across the street. . . . The lights were excruciatingly hot, and the room was stuffy. Carl stood behind his camera, staring like a mad scientist in the movies, waiting for the 'exact moment,' in which he always believed. Then the shutter began to snap, sometimes quickly, sometimes with syncopated hesitations, always with Carl's embalmed stare above. Occasionally, there were stops while the composition was improved or complicated with props: robes, costumes, banshee hats, Easter eggs, masks, feathers, cats, marionettes. . . ."

In June 1934 Van Vechten was on a holiday abroad. His main purpose in France was to visit Gertrude Stein and Alice B. Toklas at their summer residence at Bilignin in the south. Stein's famous *Autobiography of Alice B. Toklas* had been published and was reaping for its author her first popular success. Van Vechten had known both women since 1913 and had visited them a number of times. His mission now was to convince Gertrude Stein that she should accept her many offers to lecture in America in the fall. She hesitated, but by the end of Van Vechten's visit plans were in motion for the celebrated tour. During his visit Van Vechten took dozens of wonderful portraits of both women, employing the landscapes of the charming countryside, their two dogs, the rose gardens, a country church, and other natural elements. These photographs and the ones he made in New York during their subsequent visit are examples of Van Vechten's artistry at its best and are the definitive Stein-Toklas portraits.

In Paris during this same trip he renewed an old friendship with Man Ray and made a new one while photographing Salvador Dali. The session with Man Ray was mentioned by Van Vechten in his Oral History. Louis Cole,* a black dancer who had appeared in Harlem's Cotton Club revues and who was then dancing at Bricktop's Montmartre, was snapped on a Paris street, standing next to a kiosk, with vintage autos passing in the background. Three months later in New York, Van Vechten photographed Roy Atkins,* another dancer from Harlem's Cotton Club and a veteran of the *Cotton Club Parade* revues. One season he was featured with Cab Calloway* in the famous number, "The Trial on Minnie the Moocher." Van Vechten made a dramatic portrait of him seated before a textured wall-hanging resembling a sunburst.

Avon Long* had his first break in show business in the 1934 edition of the *Cotton Club Parade*. He was something new in a male dancer for the Club, where males were traditionally eccentric types, contortionistic and exhibitionistic. Long's style was smooth and subtle, though still with a jazz beat. In 1942 he performed the dancing and singing role of Sportin' Life in a revival of George Gershwin's *Porgy and Bess* at the Majestic Theatre. His performance had great authority and Virgil Thomson called the interpretation "brilliant." Two months later Van Vechten photographed him in the role.

John W. Bubbles,* of the vaudeville team of Buck and Bubbles, created the role of Sportin' Life in the original 1935 production of Gershwin's opera. He could not read music and was a doubtful choice for the character, but Gershwin had faith in him and by opening night he had mastered the role. His interpretation received wide acclaim. Naturally, Van Vechten documented his performance (December 1935).

In 1936 the most lavish of all the Cotton Club revues was staged downtown in the Palais Royale on Broadway at West 48th Street. Cab Calloway and Bill Robinson were the top-billed stars heading a cast of 130 performers. In that cast was an exotic dancer named Kaloah.* A few months earlier Van Vechten had made a series of beautiful nude studies of her. They are all I have been able to learn about her.

Beginning with Bill Robinson in 1933, Van Vechten had documented the faces and performances of many black performers. He had been intimately involved with Negroes from the days of his critical reviews of Bert Williams, George Walker, and, as early as 1913, J. Leubrie Hill, whom he reviewed in *My Friend from Kentucky*. Asadata Dafora (Horton),* an African dancer and choreographer, introduced a new kind of black theatre to New York in 1934. It was a production called *Kykunkor*, a dance-opera, which began life modestly in a hall on East 23rd Street and, under the direction of the Federal Theatre Project, moved uptown. An adaptation of African ritual in dance, costumes, and music, it reminded some critics of the Dahomey Dancers at the Chicago World's Fair of 1893. In *Kykunkor*, Dafora's faithfulness to the African heritage opened up a new era for black theatre in New York. The following year Dafora created the voodoo chants and dances for another Federal Theatre production, Orson Welles's and John Houseman's *Macbeth*. It opened in April 1936, enjoyed a long run at the Lafayette Theatre, and later toured. Welles and Houseman gave the play a Haitian setting and employed an all-Negro cast.

These two productions and Virgil Thomson's and Gertrude Stein's opera, *Four Saints in Three Acts* (1934), with an all-Negro cast, were applauded by both audiences and critics. In his article written the morning after *Four Saints* opened in Hartford's Avery Memorial Theatre on February 7, 1934 (to be followed by a run on Broadway and a later engagement in Chicago), Van Vechten emerged from retirement to call it "a rich and strange collaborative creation which very probably a future generation may be pleased to regard as a work of art." Of the dancing he said: "There are those unforgettable visions of the intricately strange prancing of the saints with torches in the second act [and] . . . the ballet of the sailors and the Spanish senoritas in the third act . . . [that] form a part of the creative staging of the piece by Frederick Ashton."

Eugene Von Grona,* a German dancer and choreographer, created the first Negro ballet company in America. His twenty-four dancers first went on the boards of Harlem's Lafayette Theatre in 1937. It was a revolutionary step for Von Grona. He had arrived in New York in the late 1920s, and for several years appeared in vaudeville, in everything from "hard labor to hot jazz" at the original Roxy Theatre and at the Palace; in 1932 he had appeared on the initial bill at the new Radio City Music Hall. The American Negro Ballet's first program included both classical and ethnic dances. The company lasted only a year because, Von Grona said, they were offered only vaudeville bookings. In March 1938 Van Vechten photographed Von Grona and Leni Bouvier* in a version of *Helen of Troy*, as well as two Negro members of the troupe, Al Bledger* and Jon Edwards,* the latter in a Firebird costume. Many of the Von Grona company went into films and some later joined Katherine Dunham.

Van Vechten has called Katherine Dunham* more a creator than a performer, and his statement is fortified by the fact that Dunham was a student of anthropology at the University of Chicago before she founded her company in New York in 1940. Certainly, as a pioneer in translating folk dance into interpretive creations she was unsurpassed during the twenty-odd years her company performed around the world. Van Vechten photographed her in 1940 and, later, members of her company: Archie Savage (1942),* Claude Marchant (1947),* and Eartha Kitt (1952).* Pearl Primus,* a dancer-choreographer who had also studied anthropology, came from a similar academic background. Arriving on the New York dance scene from Trinidad in 1943, she gave her first solo performances of her own creations based on authentic African motifs in 1943, the same year that Van Vechten photographed her in *The Blues* and other dances.

In the premiere engagement of Gian Carlo Menotti's opera, *The Medium*, Marie Powers sang the title role and Leo Coleman* danced the fascinating role of the gypsy mute, Toby. Olin Downes, in the *New York Times* for February 10, 1947, said, "[Coleman's] mute is an unforgettable figure in his facial expression of intense emotion showing inarticulately through a mask, and his amazing pantomime." Van Vechten's beautifully balanced and lighted photograph of Coleman as the mute confirms the critic's estimate of his performance.

Janet Collins* was born in New Orleans; Van Vechten photographed her shortly after she arrived in New York in 1949. The physical versatility of Collins is demonstrated in the contrast between the colorful New Orleans costume she wears in one of Van Vechten's images and a dramatic, somber view of the dancer interpreting the Negro's plight in her dance, *Nobody Knows*. She became the first black *premiere danseuse* with the Metropolitan Opera Ballet in 1951. In a letter to Bruce Kellner dated December 23, 1951, Van Vechten exclaimed that "Janet Collins . . . is a curious combination of Markova, Isadora Duncan, and Josephine Baker." A compliment indeed.

"Eloquent Alvin Ailey" was the way Van Vechten described him in an article in 1962. Ailey* began as a student with the great dance teacher, Lester Horton, in California. His first big role upon arriving in New York was in the 1955 Broadway production of *House of Flowers*. In a long series of casual, candid photographs made at this time, Van Vechten illustrated the strength, vitality, and physical beauty of the young dancer at the beginning of his career. A few years later Ailey became the founder-director of the Alvin Ailey Dance Theatre, which achieved its first successes in tours abroad in the 1960s; a German critic called the company "a triumph of sweeping, violent beauty, a furious spectacle. The stage vibrates."

Two other now-famous members of the *House of Flowers* cast were Carmen de Lavallade,* a Lester Horton student, and Geoffrey Holder,* who married de Lavallade in 1955, when Van Vechten's charming portrait of them was made. Holder had studied the native dances in his native Trinidad, and when he came to New York he taught at Katherine Dunham's school. He performed on Broadway and was a soloist with the Metropolitan Opera Ballet at the same time de Lavallade was dancing at the Metropolitan (1955). He formed his own dance company, and it is as a daring choreographer that he has received his most ardent praise, particularly for imaginative work on recent Broadway productions such as *The Wiz* and *Timbuktu!* Arthur Mitchell,* the first black dancer to be ranked as a *premier danseur* in classical ballet (with the New York City Ballet in 1959), began his career on Broadway as a modern dancer before further study changed his direction to ballet. In 1952 he appeared in the revival of the Thomson–Stein opera, *Four Saints in Three Acts*, at the Broadway Theatre. Van Vechten photographed him in a bright Hawaiian mood in 1955. Mitchell formed the Dance Theatre of Harlem in 1969, the first Negro ballet company created by a black dancer. (The Von Grona company in the 1930s had been organized by the German dancer, although the members of the company were black.)

In 1918 Van Vechten published *The Music of Spain*, the first serious work in English on the subject of Spanish music. Earlier in this introduction there are two quotations from him on the state of Spanish dancing in New York in 1915–1917; in a few words, it was almost unknown. His interest in the music of the Iberian Peninsula did not diminish, and some of his finest early photographs are of Spanish dancers. The great flamenco dancer Vicente Escudero* was before his camera in February 1933, making him one of Van Vechten's earliest subjects. As a child, Escudero had danced in the cabarets of Spain. He danced with Pavlova during the last year of her life in 1931, and in 1934 he partnered La Argentina. Later he formed his own company and toured extensively in Europe and the United States. Escudero was a gypsy dancer of great artistry, possessed of a fine sense of theatre. He choreographed works for himself and the members of his troupe.

When Van Vechten was traveling in Europe in the spring of 1935, he photographed a variety of gypsies from the Granada and Sevilla districts, the dance centers in Spain. The photograph I have chosen is one of three anonymous female gypsy dancers from the legendary Sacro-Monte in Granada.* The figure lines and the contrasts in light and shadow give the photograph almost the quality of a painting. Van Vechten photographed the Mexican dancer and choreographer, José Fernandez,* in 1939. In our photograph the dancer is performing the bulerías from a New York revue called *Mexicana*. Later Fernandez joined the first season of Ballet Theatre, choreographing the Spanish repertory. In 1947 Fernandez and Lew Christensen choreographed *Pastorela*, an opera-ballet with music by Paul Bowles, first produced by Ballet Society.

In October 1940, Van Vechten had the good fortune of being able to photograph a series of dramatic and definitive studies of the greatest interpreter of Spanish dancing in her time, Argentinita.* The first artist to treat the folk dances of Central and South America in a creative way, she was graceful and poised in her dancing technique while retaining the essential rhythms in the music. She gained her fame in recitals rather than in the more usual revue or cabaret performances. Argentinita's last two partners were José Greco and Manolo Vargas. Her last American appearance was as a guest artist with Ballet Theatre at the Metropolitan Opera House in April 1945. Still at the peak of her career, she died later the same year at the age of forty-seven. Edwin Denby has said of Argentinita: "More than any other dancer, she made the Spanish style easy for North Americans to appreciate and enjoy." Van Vechten's fine studio photographs of her are a lasting tribute to her artistry.

Less dramatic than the Argentinita portraits, but a beautifully balanced camera study, is Van Vechten's image of Carmen Vazquez and Miguel Herrero in a scene from *Cabalgata*,* a Spanish revue produced in 1949.

Although most of the dancers Van Vechten photographed in the early years were from Broadway or from ethnic companies, an exception was Charles Weidman, photographed in December 1933. The first dancer associated with the ballet to sit for him was William Dollar.* In the April 1935 photograph, Dollar is seen in costume from the Balanchine revival of *Errante*, produced by the American Ballet. This was early in Dollar's career, before he had made his name as a leading American dancer; arthritis shortened his career, but he went on to further distinction as a choreographer. His best ballet, *Le Combat* (1949), has been honored by performances in the repertories of both Ballet Theatre and the New York City Ballet.

The strong, masculine face of Adolph Bolm* was photographed by Van Vechten in the spring of 1937. He was a link to the past, since he had been Pavlova's first great partner in 1907-1908 and was *premier danseur* in Diaghilev's company, heading the Russian Ballet company in its first tour in 1909-1910. After the company's second American tour Bolm remained in Chicago and formed the Ballet Intime with Ruth Page in 1917. Between 1933 and 1939 he was ballet master for the San Francisco Opera Ballet; in 1940 he joined Ballet Theatre in its initial season, and worked with them again in 1942-1943. Bolm staged Stravinsky's *Firebird* for Ballet Theatre in 1945, with Alicia Markova and Anton Dolin in the principal roles.

In 1938 Van Vechten made a fascinating series of studio photographs of Wilbur McCormick* in his famous "Boxing" dance, a sequence from *Olympiad: A Sports Suite*, itself a part of Ted Shawn's *O, Libertad!* McCormick had been captain of a wrestling team before he joined Ted Shawn and his men dancers in 1933, the year the Shawn company was organized. He was a leading dancer from the first season and remained with the company for all seven of its celebrated tours, until it disbanded in 1940, and most of the members entered the military services in World War II. The company toured throughout the United States, Canada, and Cuba, and performed in London in the spring of 1935. The masculine image that McCormick and the other Shawn dancers projected through their muscular dancing and Shawn's powerful choreography contributed much to a general acceptance of male dancers by American audiences.

An athlete of a vastly different nature was Gilda Gray,* the Polish dancer credited with inventing the "shimmy" dance. It brought her to fame on Broadway in *Hello Alexander* (1919) and the *Ziegfeld Follies of 1922*, in which she shared billing with Vivienne Segal and Gallagher & Shean. In the mid-twenties Gray was a star in vaudeville and made several appearances in Hollywood films. Van Vechten photographed her in her famous shimmy costume at Billy Rose's Diamond Horseshoe during the New York World's Fair in 1940.

Some of the most beautiful and exotic camera studies Van Vechten ever made were of the Indian dancer, Ram Gopal,* performing his authentic Hindu dances. The long series of Gopal performance poses were completed on various days during April and May 1938. Gopal was already a legend. He had opened an Indian classical dancing school in Bangalore, India, in 1935, when he was fifteen years old, and had just arrived in America when Van Vechten photographed him. Gopal later toured Europe and after World War II visited both continents again and taught and danced at Jacob's Pillow during the 1950s.

Van Vechten's first major venture into the public eye with his photographic work was an exhibit at the Second International Leica Exhibition of Photography in November 1935. The other photographers in the show were Cecil Beaton, George Platt Lynes, Man Ray, and Edward Steichen. Critic Henry McBride said: "What is literature's loss is photography's gain—quite distinctly Mr. Van Vechten is the Bronzino of this camera period."

During his first decade spent pursuing the art, Van Vechten photographed movers and shakers in the literary, art, sports, and theatre worlds, as well as the dancers—a catholic collection, though the concentration was on literary figures. He recorded many of the roles performed by Judith Anderson, shot a continuing series of camera studies of Eugene O'Neill, and, of course, took many photographs of Gertrude Stein and Alice B. Toklas, in both France and New York. In fact, he documented Stein's journey to Richmond, Virginia, in 1934, when she spoke at the University and was lavishly admired and entertained by the local intelligentsia.

Adolph Bolm, 1937

The Gertrude Stein photographic episode was intense but brief compared to his new devotion to Ballet Theatre. In its first decade (1940–1950) he made a subjective photographic history of the company and the works it premiered. He was usually successful in securing the dancer first associated with a role, frequently recording it within a few days following the opening night. Ballet Theatre holds a unique position in United States dance history. In a few months of concentrated organization in the late 1930s, a directorial board was formed, funds were raised, and a company of dancers and choreographers brought together. They opened a first season in January 1940 to immediate popular and critical acclaim. This exciting project was exactly calculated to intrigue Van Vechten, and he immediately poured his enthusiasm and encouragement for the new Ballet Theatre into action by being on hand from the first night and arranging for his documentation of the company's progress on film.

In his Oral History in 1960, Van Vechten recalled the period of the birth of Ballet Theatre: "Nineteen-Forty has so many things in it . . . the years 1940 to 1950 . . . that I hardly know how to begin. Color film was invented and was on the market around 1938 and I began using it in 1939. I took an exhaustive series of the World's Fair at Flushing, and almost immediately I began taking pictures of the ballet. I began knowing ballet people, and I took a very long series that went on all through 1940 and on through the 1950s of Alicia Markova,* who is probably the greatest living exponent of the ballet. This is shown frequently—they're exposed on the screen—color pictures of her in practically all of her roles that I took from 1940 to late in the fifties."

When the interviewer asked if color film suggested to Van Vechten that he photograph ballet, he replied: "I had been talking ballet and going to ballet ever since I saw the Russian dancers in 1910 or 1911, but the color film gave me an extra outlook on it. I could do things I hadn't done before. The pictures of the ballet went on extensively, with many other people. . . ."

Van Vechten was laying plans for the disposition of all his photographic work. Certain institutions were logical choices, based on subject matter. He was always interested in creative Negroes in all the arts and founded two collections to preserve his photographs of them: the Rose McClendon Memorial Collection of Photographs by Carl Van Vechten of Celebrated Negroes, housed at Howard University, and the Jerome Bowers Peterson Memorial Collection of Photographs by Carl Van Vechten of Notable Negroes, located at the University of New Mexico. At Fisk University he founded the George Gershwin Memorial Collection of Music and Musical Literature in 1946. This impressive collection included letters, scores, manuscripts, programs, and photographs of music and dance personalities. Portraits of theatrical personalities are housed at the Museum of the City of New York; the Museum of Modern Art holds a collection of his photographs of dancers and choreographers. The Beinecke Library at Yale contains in the Carl Van Vechten Collection his American correspondence, including many photographs and all the extant negatives for the entire Van Vechten photographic record. Also at Yale is the James Weldon Johnson Collection of Negro Arts and Letters, founded by Van Vechten in 1941, containing a large collection of manuscripts, correspondence, and photographs of Negroes in all the arts. In the Dance Collection of the New York Public Library at Lincoln Center for the Performing Arts are more than 5,000 Van Vechten photographs of dancers and choreographers, presented in honor of Van Vechten's actress wife, Fania Marinoff. They are an integral part of the Lincoln Center dance holdings.

The largest single collection of Van Vechten photographs is housed in the Philadelphia Museum of Art, presented to the Museum by the late Mark Lutz. Lutz had been a close friend and associate since 1931, and had assisted Van Vechten with his camera work in the early days. Thereafter he became the recipient of copies of all the photographs the photographer wished to be preserved. The Philadelphia collection numbers 13,000 images, representing the entire scope of his work. Lutz presented the collection to the Museum shortly before his own death in 1968.

Photographing a single dancer or group of dancers in a particular work was not always an easy task. The complications increased as Van Vechten grew more eager to capture on film the desired person at the proper time. This included other companies performing in New York in addition to the Ballet Theatre repertory. In the Oral History he comments on the problems: "I take photographs very often definitely for certain collections. But it doesn't always follow, because when you're photographing, you have to take what's available, you see. Getting people to be photographed is not as simple as it sounds. It was easier for me at first, when I was only a friend and had no axe to grind. Now that I want certain people definitely to fill in, sometimes it's very hard to get them because I don't know them very well, or they don't understand about the collections. Being photographed is an awful job, you know. It's not easy. Sometimes I have people up here for hours, in various costumes and so forth. It takes time. I'm very particular, and I want certain backgrounds. I want all sorts of things. When Markova was being photographed, she was sometimes here all night. That happened with many people. . . ."

By the fall of 1942 the Van Vechten archive was impressive. Since his first show seven years earlier in 1935, his name as a photographer had become widely known. Many of his portraits had been reproduced in books and magazines. *Theatre Arts* magazine, in its August 1942 "Negro Theatre" issue, had featured many of his camera studies, and in its December 1942 issue had published a full-page portrait of dancer Hugh Laing in *Goya Pasto-*

rale.* In October 1943 *Theatre Arts* included a portfolio of four pages of Van Vechten studies of Markova accompanying an article on the ballerina. The Museum of the City of New York gave him a one-man show, "The Theatre through the Camera of Carl Van Vechten," which opened on November 18, 1942. It totaled more than 100 photographs. The invitation to the exhibition read: "An array of stage and screen stars, playwrights, scene designers, singers, composers and dancers covering the last ten years."

The success of Ballet Theatre was the result of a series of fortuitous events as well as disciplined planning. Mikhail Mordkin had danced with Pavlova at the Metropolitan Opera House in 1910 in *Coppélia.* Van Vechten, as the dance critic for the *Times*, described their performances: "Such dancing has not been seen on the local stage during the present generation." In 1937 Mordkin organized his Mordkin Ballet as an outlet for his more talented students. The next year it became a professional company dancing his versions of *Giselle, La Fille Mal Gardée*, and other standard ballets. Accepting the financial aid donated by his former student, Lucia Chase, and utilizing the talents of publicity genius Richard Pleasant, the trio created Ballet Theatre in 1939. Pleasant insured success by bringing Antony Tudor* from England as resident choreographer; through the efforts of these four talented people, Ballet Theatre was born. Mordkin remained active with the new company for only one season and then returned to teaching.

The first Ballet Theatre season opened January 11, 1940, at the Center Theatre, with a program of *Les Sylphides*, Mordkin's *Voices of Spring*, and Eugene Loring's *The Great American Goof.* During the first season Tudor's *Jardin aux Lilas,* later called *Lilac Garden*, was premiered, with Hugh Laing* and Tudor in their original roles from the English production of 1936. Although Viola Essen was the first Caroline in the Ballet Theatre production, Nora Kaye* was later known for the role.

The world premiere of *Black Ritual** took place on January 22. A daring venture using all Negro dancers, it displayed Agnes de Mille in her debut with this company as a choreographer and was set to music by Darius Milhaud. This was the first complete ballet that Van Vechten photographed. Historically a pioneering work for de Mille and the company, although it had only three performances, it was the first time Negroes had worked in so ambitious a production. De Mille in her autobiography said that since the Negro dancers performed in no other work, they were considered a luxury for the new company, so "my girls were dispersed and the work has never since been performed."

Tudor's *Judgment Of Paris,* with music by Kurt Weill, was first performed in London in 1938 with de Mille, Tudor, and Laing. They repeated their roles in the New York production. The first season's last major premiere was Tudor's *Dark Elegies,* music by Gustav Mahler, and danced by Laing, Tudor, and Chase. Van Vechten captured de Mille, Tudor, Laing, and others from the roster with his lens. De Mille in her autobiography says, "Carl Van Vechten, who remembers well, has stated that there were dancers performing solos for Diaghilev that could not have passed our first chorus auditions."

An innovation for the second season at the Majestic Theatre was the omission of a stage manager, or *regisseur.* Indeed, the company was divided into parts: Anton Dolin* (summoned from England) was in charge of the classical repertory; Tudor organized the English wing; and Loring was in command of the American section. The season opened on February 11, 1941, with Tudor's *Gala Performance*, with Tudor, Laing, Kaye, and Nana Gollner in the cast. A highlight of the second season was the premiere of de Mille's *Three Virgins and a Devil,* with Respighi's music. De Mille* danced the role of the Priggish Virgin, Chase* was the Greedy Virgin, and Annabelle Lyon* was the Lustful one. Loring danced the role of the Devil and Jerome Robbins* had his first principal role as a Youth. The ballet and its cast excited Van Vechten into recreating it on film in his studio.

Richard Pleasant resigned his position as director of Ballet Theatre in the summer of 1941, leaving Lucia Chase to reorganize the company with a changing roster of directors until 1945, when she and Oliver Smith* became codirectors. Impressario S. Hurok was hired to book the company's third season beginning in November at the 44th Street Theatre. In order to popularize the company in the eyes of the public, Hurok emphasized in advertising and press releases that although Ballet Theatre was American, it was artistically Russian in character. It was felt that American audiences, especially outside of New York, were not ready to accept ballet as an American product. The company had toured after both the first and second seasons, and the Russian selling point was affirmed. However, the repertory added more American works and performers each season. In time, as we know, the dance public accepted the ballet as international and the Russian publicity was dropped. Hurok left his position with the company during the summer of 1946.

The November 1941 season followed an engagement in Mexico City. Ballet Theatre continued introducing repertory interpreted by a company gaining an international reputation. The season opened with the American premiere of Fokine's *Bluebeard,* with music by Offenbach, decor by Marcel Vertes,* and Markova, Kaye, Dolin, Ian Gibson, and Tudor in principal roles. Dolin's *Princess Aurora* (Aurora's Wedding),* the last act of *Sleeping Beauty*, premiered with Irina Baronova, partnered by Dolin. Markova and Gibson* later alternated in the roles. After another tour the company opened at the Metropolitan Opera House in April 1942 with Tudor's *Pillar of Fire,* to music by Arnold Schönberg. Nora Kaye* danced Hagar: it was the role that transformed

Antony Tudor, Hugh Laing, and Carl Van Vechten, 1940

her into a great dramatic ballerina. Chase, Lyon, Laing, and Tudor completed the cast.

Ballet Theatre premiered Leonide Massine's *Aleko,** with Tchaikovsky's music and sets and costumes by Marc Chagall,* at the Metropolitan in the fall of 1942, after summer warm-ups in Mexico City. Markova,* Laing,* and Tudor were the principals; Kaye alternated with Markova in the role of Zemphira. It was a departure for Markova after mastering the classic *Giselle** and *Swan Lake*; her Zemphira was a gypsy described by critic Grace Robert as "quite [a] different sort of dramatic intensity . . . with sunburnt make-up, wild hair, and a vivid red costume . . . [her] authoritative dancing style, now turned to the uses of *demi-caractère*." *Petrouchka** was restaged by Fokine, and there were revivals of Loring's *Billy The Kid,** music by Aaron Copland* and sets and costumes by Jared French* (in which Van Vechten photographed John Kriza* and Donald Saddler*), and Dolin's *Swan Lake,** with its imaginative sets by Lee Simonson.*

In the spring of 1943, again at the Metropolitan, Tudor's *Romeo and Juliet,** with Laing and Markova dancing the title roles, was premiered. In the fall Kaye and Laing created Tudor's *Dim Lustre.** Jerome Robbins offered his first choreographic creation in April 1944, with the now-classic *Fancy Free.** It was an instant success, from its inspired score by Leonard Bernstein* and lively sets by Oliver Smith to its near-perfect cast of Robbins himself, Harold Lang, and John Kriza* as three sailors on leave in New York and Janet Reed, Muriel Bentley, and Shirley Eckl as "passersby." Van Vechten called it "a masterpiece from beginning to end." Since its premiere many dancers have interpreted the roles, with varying success. *Fancy Free* remains one of the most popular American ballets. It was in the repertory of Ballet Theatre exclusively until 1980, when Robbins restaged it for the New York City Ballet. The spring of 1944 also saw de Mille's *Tally-Ho,** with de Mille in the first performances with Laing. Janet Reed* later essayed her role.

During the first several seasons of Ballet Theatre four names dominated the company as choreographers and dancers. All had been major dance names in England before they joined the New York company. Antony Tudor, a leading choreographer and dancer, pointed the direction of the company in the early years. Hugh Laing, who introduced many of the Tudor roles, had been a favorite dancer in England. He remained with Ballet Theatre for all but one year in its first decade. In 1945-1946 he appeared in the Broadway musical, *The Day before Spring*, for which Tudor created the dances. Only slightly less influential during this time was Anton Dolin, who presided over and danced much of the classical repertory. A *premier danseur* in England, he founded and was director of the Markova-Dolin Ballet from 1935 to 1938. In 1941 Alicia Markova came to the United States and joined Ballet Theatre during its second season.

Van Vechten immediately recognized in Alicia Markova a creative performing artist who richly deserved her designation as *prima ballerina assoluta*. He recorded her roles on film as she introduced them with Ballet Theatre and other companies. In an article Van Vechten wrote for *Esquire* (December 1962), he said: "[In 1941] I started a series, with *Giselle,** of Alicia Markova in her best-known roles." When the series was completed in 1955, Van Vechten had photographed Markova in twenty-four ballets during the years of her greatest artistry. These hundreds of photographs by a single photographer constitute one of the most exhaustive photographic records of the art of a ballerina that has been achieved. In his late years Van Vechten would gather an appreciative audience in his apartment in the San Remo on Central Park West and spend an evening showing color slides of the ballerina whom he called, in his introduction to Markova's autobiography, *Giselle and I* (1960), "the greatest figure on the contemporary dancing stage . . . one of the greatest of all time."

In a letter to the artist George George (July 5, 1943), Van Vechten wrote of Markova and other ballerinas: "Markova, it is highly probable, is the greatest classical dancer of all time, not only greater than Pavlova (far, far greater), but greater than Taglioni. I *know* she is greater than Pavlova because I have seen Pavlova countless times. It is fairly simple to deduct she is greater than Taglioni because, even since Pavlova's time, technique has advanced so rapidly that dancers are required to do things now (with ease and to the manner born) that no dancer of 20 years ago would have attempted. Pavlova had an inner grace, a 'soul,' a poetic approach, but she is excelled even in this department by the exquisite Alicia, who like Ariel, appears to be sexless."

Ballet Theatre enjoyed great loyalty from its members as well as from its patrons during these early years, contributing to the company's continuing successes. It is interesting that this success came despite the fact that the company never enjoyed a permanent theatre as a home base of operations. Its rival company, the New York City Ballet, was housed at one time (when it was called American Ballet) at the Metropolitan Opera House, and later operated from the New York City Center until April 1964, when it moved into the new New York State Theater at Lincoln Center.

J. Alden Talbot resigned as the last of a series of directors for Ballet Theatre in the spring of 1945; Lucia Chase and Oliver Smith became codirectors. The departure of Talbot, and of Hurok a year later, contributed to the change in Ballet Theatre's image from a classical Russian company to a renewed version of the company as it had begun in 1940, creating from within its own roster of choreographers. Tudor's *Undertow* (1945), danced by Laing and Nana Gollner, though traditional in its classical form, has been called "a modern psychological ballet" in content. The fall 1945 season also included

Alicia Markova and Carl Van Vechten, 1943

Michael Kidd's *On Stage!* and Robbins's *Interplay*, with decor by Smith and costumes by Irene Sharaff,* and danced by Kaye, Reed, Bentley, Melissa Hayden, Kriza, and Lang. It was a themeless work, although the interpretation could only be described as pure American. In July and August 1946 Ballet Theatre played the Royal Opera House Covent Garden, London, with André Eglevsky and Kaye as leading soloists; it was a great success. Ballet Theatre was the first American company to tour Europe after World War II.

In October Ballet Theatre premiered, at the Broadway Theatre, Robbins's *Facsimile*,* with a score by Bernstein, sets by Smith, and costumes by Sharaff. Kaye, Kriza, and Robbins danced the opening performance, the latter shortly replaced by Laing. Robbins left Ballet Theatre after this production and joined the newly reorganized New York City Ballet. Tudor was named artistic administrator of the company. Tudor had been a vital part of the operations of Ballet Theatre from the beginning, and remained so for a decade until he left the company in 1950. As a choreographer he preferred the "interesting" dancer to the technically perfect one, and he demanded the use of a dancer's total body rather than conventional mime as a means of expression. Both Nora Kaye and Hugh Laing fit this description and remained the finest interpreters of his ballets.

One of de Mille's most famous creations was *Fall River Legend*,* based on the legendary Lizzie Borden story. Ballet Theatre premiered it at the Metropolitan in 1948—music by Morton Gould and appropriately stark decor by Oliver Smith. De Mille created the role of Lizzie for Nora Kaye, who was ill for the first performances, when it was danced by Alicia Alonso. Kaye later danced Lizzie to great personal success; John Kriza created the role of the pastor. The ballet has been hailed as one of the great American ballets by critics and audiences in the United States and abroad ever since it first was performed.

The last Ballet Theatre production that Van Vechten photographed by recreating it in his studio was Tudor's *Shadow of the Wind*,* with music by Mahler, based on eighth-century poems by Li Po. The 1948 production had a large cast including Gollner,* Bentley,* Diana Adams,* Laing,* and Eric Braun.* Although it was not a popular success, it is historically important since it represents Tudor's last major work of that period with Ballet Theatre. After 1950 Tudor became a teacher at the Metropolitan Opera Ballet School and only in recent years has he returned on occasion to create new material for the ballet.

In the fall of 1950 Ballet Theatre became for one season the official company of the Metropolitan Opera. At this time the company lost Adams, Kaye, and Laing to New York City Ballet. Ballet Theatre became American Ballet Theatre at the time of a 1957 tour to the Near East and Europe.

By the end of its first decade, Van Vechten had made thousands of photographs of Ballet Theatre's repertory, its dancers and choreographers. In his studio he had recreated *Black Ritual, Judgment of Paris, Three Virgins and a Devil, Shadow of the Wind, Fall River Legend*, and others. He had photographed his favorite performers in personal portraits and in their roles. Around 1950 he lost interest in Ballet Theatre as a company, the most obvious reason being that Kaye, Laing, Adams, and others of his favorites had defected to the New York City Ballet. Kaye, Laing, and Markova remained his three favorite photographic subjects. Markova had danced as a company member, but often only as a guest artist; she divided her time among several ballet companies, both in the United States and abroad. She also toured extensively with Anton Dolin, her favorite partner.

During the same years, Van Vechten had photographed dancers from other companies in addition to Ballet Theatre, particularly Ballet Russe de Monte Carlo, Ballet Caravan, Ballet International, Ballet Society, and the New York City Ballet. In 1940 he recorded George Zoritch* in his role in Massine's *Gaîté Parisienne* in the Ballet Russe production. He accomplished a beautiful set of camera studies of Tatiana Riabouchinska* in Fokine's *Les Sylphides* for the Ballet Russe (1942). For the Ballet Society production of Balanchine's *The Four Temperaments*, he photographed Todd Bolender (1947).*

The Marquis George de Cuevas's Ballet International, in its first season in 1944, presented Edward Caton's *Sebastian*,* with music by Gian-Carlo Menotti and decor by Oliver Smith, at the International Theatre (originally the Park Theatre) located on Columbus Circle. Francisco Moncion* created the title role (his first major assignment), Viola Essen* was the Courtesan, and Kari Karnakoski* was the Prince. Van Vechten photographed them all against fantastic backgrounds in his studio, emphasizing the unusual costumes and the fantasy elements of the ballet's setting in seventeenth-century Venice. That same fall Van Vechten photographed André Eglevsky,* the great classical dancer, in the American premiere of the Romanov-Rubinstein *Prince Goudal's Festival*, also presented by Ballet International.

During World War II Van Vechten was a captain at the Stage Door Canteen and, of course, documented his activities there with hundreds of photographs. Among the most delightful is a 1942 series of action shots of dancer Frank "Killer Joe" Piro,* at that time a sailor, jitterbugging with a young, vivacious hostess, Shirley Booth.* Another departure from traditional dance subjects that intrigued Van Vechten were the ice-skating variations on classical dance in Sonja Henie's ice revues. He photographed Harrison Thomson* as Prince Charming in a *Sleeping Beauty* ballet on ice in 1947, and Thomson and Rudy Richards* in the revue, *Howdy, Mr. Ice*, a year later.

In September 1948 Van Vechten documented a performance in what may be the finest set of dance images to emerge from his studio. The Ballet Russe de Monte Carlo mounted Jules Perrot's legendary *Pas de Quatre*,* reconstructed by Anton Dolin. It was danced to music by Cesare Pugni and was originally performed on July 12, 1845, by Fanny Cerito, Lucile Grahn, Carlotta Grisi, and Maria Taglioni, the four greatest ballerinas of their day. It had been the remarkable feat of Benjamin Lumley, director of Her Majesty's Theatre, London, to secure the services of such luminaries for the first performance. Dolin, inspired by the famous lithograph by A.E. Chalon, produced the ballet first in 1941 for Ballet Theatre, followed regularly through the decade with varying casts. The most notable was the production by Ballet Russe de Monte Carlo at the Metropolitan Opera House, September 18, 1948, with Alexandra Danilova (Cerito),* Nathalie Krassovska (Grahn),* Mia Slavenska (Grisi),* and Alicia Markova (Taglioni).* The resulting photographs by Van Vechten are equal to the poetic beauty of the artist's rendering of the glorious nineteenth-century originals.

Van Vechten made his last Atlantic crossing to Europe in 1949. The first had been in 1907, and he had returned to Paris as correspondent for the *New York Times* (1908–1909), discovering the beauty and wonders of the City of Light before most of the famous expatriates who followed him in the next two decades. During a 1913 visit he made two major discoveries: Gertrude Stein and Igor Stravinsky. He attended the legendary first performances of Stravinsky's *Le Sacre du Printemps* (choreographed by Nijinsky) in May 1913. His version of the evening is among the most celebrated of the many penned about the event: "A certain part of the audience, thrilled by what it considered a blasphemous attempt to destroy music as an art, and swept away with wrath, began very soon after the rise of the curtain to whistle, to make catcalls, and to offer audible suggestions as to how the performance should proceed. Others of us, who liked the music and felt that the principles of free speech were at stake, bellowed defiance. It was war over art for the rest of the evening and the orchestra played on unheard, except occasionally when a slight lull occurred. The figures on the stage danced in time to music they had to imagine they heard and beautifully out of rhythm with the uproar in the auditorium. I was sitting in a box in which I had rented one seat. Three ladies sat in front of me and a young man occupied the place behind me. He stood up during the course of the ballet to enable himself to see more clearly. The intense excitement under which he was laboring, thanks to the potent force of the music, betrayed itself presently when he began to beat rhythmically on the top of my head with his fists. My emotion was so great that I did not feel the blows for some time. They were perfectly synchronized with the beat of the music. When I did, I turned around. His apology was sincere.

We had both been carried beyond ourselves."

In the 1920s and 1930s he visited England, France, Italy, and Spain several times. In 1949, nearing seventy, he made the final journey to Paris, at which time he photographed Jean Cocteau, Jean Marais, Andre Maurois, and, of course, Alice B. Toklas. At the Folies Bergère he saw Josephine Baker* and made a photographic portrait of her in one of her glamorous dancing gowns. On the same evening he took an informal picture of her emerging from the theatre after the performance. Two years later (spring 1951) he photographed Baker in her dressing room at the Strand Theatre in New York, during her triumphant engagement that preceded several successful United States tours.

Van Vechten departed from the ballet to photograph the Broadway dances created by de Mille for the Frederick Loewe and Alan Jay Lerner musical, *Paint Your Wagon*,* which opened at the Shubert Theatre (November 12, 1951) with James Barton and Olga San Juan heading the cast. In a series of photographs he captured the western motif displayed in the colorful costumes by Motley and in the spirited dancing by James Mitchell,* Mary Burr,* Tamara Chapman,* and Dorothy Hill.* Arthur Todd in *Theatre Arts* (November 1951) said that Broadway "needed a de Mille to further mesh the ballet with the book in a way that would 'move' and animate an entire production. . . . Her knowledge of what was good for her developed a marvelous sense of characterization that has been one of the dominant characteristics in her composing for the concert, ballet, and Broadway theatre fields."

Only a month before the opening of *Paint Your Wagon*, Van Vechten observed in a letter to Bruce Kellner (October 11, 1951): "It is curious, but while singers and actors have deteriorated, violinists, pianists, and ballerinas in every department have improved. Indeed, the whole technique of the ballet has changed to a terrific extent. So, whereas I used to frequently attend the opera, now I spend my evenings at the ballet, when it is around." In another letter to Kellner (February 27, 1952) he commented on Tudor's *La Gloire*, danced by his favorites Adams, Kaye, Laing, and Moncion for the New York City Ballet: "The ballet is so good that the critics are beginning to demand perfection." It was not a popular work, however, and was shortly dropped from the repertory. It was one of only two ballets that Antony Tudor created for the New York City Ballet, the other being *Lady of the Camellias.*

A reflection voiced by Van Vechten in a letter to Kellner on April 5, 1952, seems ironic today, with so many dancers defecting from Russia to the West: "The New York City Ballet flies to Barcelona on April 7 and it is there they open their European tour. There have been repercussions about their appearing first in a fascist country, but dancers know little of politics and care less,

GOOD dancers, that is. Some dancers are more politicians than dancers."

In the fall of 1952 Van Vechten made a series of exquisite photographs of two Balinese dancers, with much excitement at the time and eventual personal satisfaction. In a letter to Kellner on September 24, he transferred his feelings to paper: "The Balinese dancers are out of this world, incredibly beautiful in color and movement, incredibly different. They are like nothing earthly. The leading dancer (Ni Gusti Raka)* is 9 years old and I can't tell you how exciting she is. I am trying to photograph her and Sampih,* the leading male dancer. Girls are pretty much finished as dancers when they reach the ripe age of 13; men seemingly go on forever, tho' Sampih is perhaps about 30. I have heard of these dancers . . . for a long time, but the reality is greater than the anticipation. The comic dancers, too, who howl, the grotesque animals, are wonderful on a different plane. The Barong ends with this delightful creature devouring everybody on the stage."

The New York City Ballet mounted a revival of the Lincoln Kirstein-Lew Christensen ballet, *Filling Station*, with music by Virgil Thomson,* at City Center in May 1953. Van Vechten photographed Michael Maule* in the role of the Rich Boy. Maule toured as partner to Danilova (1954–1956), and partnered Markova in the 1958 Metropolitan Opera production of Glück's opera, *Orfeo ed Euridice.*

Iris Mabry* was a contemporary modern dancer who choreographed all her own material. Van Vechten discovered her in 1954 and after seeing her for the first time wrote a delightful vignette to Kellner on March 7: "Did you ever by any chance see Iris Mabry dance? She is the sister of one of my best friends, but I had never seen her until night before last when I drew on my bearskin coat and my skunk hat, jumped aboard my sled and was dragged by dog team to the center of Brooklyn, which I was amazed to discover belongs to the United States. Anyway, tho she has faults and her husband's [Ralph Gilbert] music, which she employs exclusively, is pretty poor, she is amazing. The most beautiful of bodies in skintight dresses or leotards without a wrinkle. Extraordinary movements, powerfully or gracefully executed, and quite astounding technique (according to her lights which included bare feet—NOT on points)."

Alicia Markova and Milorad Miskovitch* toured England, France, and the United States in a 1954 concert engagement performing Fokine's *Dying Swan** and Debussy's *L'Après-midi d'un Faune,** among other works. The latter was an adaptation honoring the 25th anniversary of Diaghilev's death; Miskovitch dancing the role created by Nijinsky. Van Vechten, keeping his record of Markova's career up to date, photographed them in his studio.

Melissa Hayden* began her professional career as a member of the Radio City Music Hall corps de ballet. She joined Ballet Theatre in 1945 and moved on to New York City Ballet in 1950, remaining there except for occasional guest appearances with other companies. Van Vechten had been full of praise for her dancing from the beginning, but somehow did not photograph her until 1956. However, in his letters to Kellner he frequently expresses his feelings for her artistry. For example, on March 26, 1956: "The ballet of the year, or almost any year, turned out to be *The Still Point* by Todd Bolender with Melissa Hayden (who couldn't be greater, more exciting, more tender, or more generally lovely) and Jacques d'Amboise. I expected so little of this that I did not have tickets for it and only got in by appealing to Lincoln Kirstein at the last matinee as the house was completely sold out. I shivered and shook and sobbed aloud, and I dare say I bled."

(December 18, 1958) "An evening at the ballet last week was the most brilliant performance of ballet I have ever seen anywhere. *Medea* (choreographed by Birgit Cullberg) was absolutely terrific. This is probably Melissa's greatest performance. . . . From costumes, music [Bartók] to conductor and dancers, it is as much perfection as one encounters. D'Amboise and [Violette] Verdy* are only a little behind Melissa and it is probably d'Amboise at his best too. . . ."

Critic Don McDonagh has said that "modern dance consists of intelligent approaches to movement, the approaches designed to create significant form." A pioneer in carrying out this idea is dancer and choreographer Paul Taylor.* A disciplined performer, he is best known for the experimental solo and group dances he has created. Clive Barnes has admiringly called Taylor "a fantastic choreographer." Taylor began his career as a dancer with the Merce Cunningham company in 1953, and in the following year formed his own company. He was a leading soloist with Martha Graham from 1955 to 1961 and created the role of Aegisthus in Graham's *Clytemnestra* and The Destroyer In *Samson Agonistes.* His individuality and skill as a showman appealed to Van Vechten as well as to audiences. He was photographed by Van Vechten (1960) in his whimsical work, *The Least Flycatcher,** and in the variation that Balanchine created for him in *Episodes** for the New York City Ballet. Balanchine's solo was designed to display the dancer's formidable athletic figure and muscular command; the variation has not been performed by any other dancer.

In the 1930s and 1940s Martha Graham* worked virtually alone in her pursuit of developing what we call modern dance. Later she was fortunate in having as her collaborators talented people such as lighting and production designer Jean Rosenthal,* designer Isamu Noguchi,* and composer Louis Horst. Her dance origins began in 1917 with the Denishawn company, as did those of many American dancers. In 1923 she ended her apprenticeship with Denishawn and emerged with ideas of her own. After engagements with the *Greenwich Village*

Martha Graham and Carl Van Vechten at the 44th Street Theatre, 1962
Photo courtesy of Martha Swope.

Follies and other revues, she began her own experimental creations. By the 1950s her revolutionary work had become an important part of the American modern dance scene. Van Vechten seems not to have been moved by Graham in the early years of her career, and it was only in 1961 that he photographed her. By this time he had joined the growing throngs of her admirers. In a letter to me on October 27, 1963, he said: "Yesterday I attended Martha Graham's dances for the second time; I am more than ever impressed by this lady. I believe her to be the greatest living choreographer."

He photographed Graham and Bertram Ross in what is probably her greatest achievement, *Clytemnestra* (1961).* The set was designed by Isamu Noguchi, the Japanese-American sculptor who had worked with Graham since 1934. *Clytemnestra* had the unique distinction of being the first three-act modern dance work. Van Vechten made a long series of studio-recreated action images of Graham and Ross in *Visionary Recital*,* another important Graham work, which was retitled *Samson Agonistes* in its revised version. Thus far, Graham has created over 145 dance works. Graham and Ross were the last important dancers that Van Vechten was to capture through his lens.

John Martin,* the dance critic for the *New York Times* between 1927 and 1962, sat for Van Vechten in 1956. In many ways Martin was Van Vechten's descendant, and he praised the older critic's early writings on the dance for making his own reviews more acceptable to readers. Martin, certainly the most influential dance critic during his tenure with the *Times*, said of Van Vechten, one month after his death: "Everyone who 'did' anything publicly—actors, writers, musicians, prize fighters, all sorts of dancers, painters, jazz singers—he knew, photographed and corresponded with, until he amassed a virtual montage of the public face of performance focused through a private and personal eye."

Lincoln Kirstein,* cofounder of the School of American Ballet (1934), founder of Ballet Caravan (1936), founder of the Dance Archive of the Museum of Modern Art (1940), founder-editor of *Dance Index* and *Hound and Horn*, cofounder of Ballet Society (1946), and since 1948 general director of New York City Ballet, is an outstanding American authority on dance. His contributions to the dance field are endless. It was in May 1933 that the twenty-six-year-old Kirstein first sat for Van Vechten, as one of the photographer's earliest subjects. The result of that sitting was a chiaroscuro study in light and shadow; Van Vechten was experimenting with his new profession and had not yet settled upon the stylistic factors that later distinguished a Van Vechten photograph from all others. It is a splendid portrait, flattering to both the subject and the photographer. In November 1964 Kirstein again sat for the photographer, and was the last person Van Vechten photographed. It is a fine portrait, and the thirty-one years separating the two pictures have been kind, indeed, to the sitter.

A historian on the dance, Kirstein had known Van Vechten since 1926, and after the latter's death on December 21, 1964, wrote a touching tribute to his friend for the Yale Library *Gazette* of April 1965: "Carl Van Vechten told me and taught me many things, the most important being a sense of the individual, idiosyncratic authority of elegance as style. . . . [He] saw the surprising in the ordinary; he found, perhaps first in any articulate degree, the natural flair, the talent for rhythm and expressiveness, the joy, the fire, the murder, and the verbal accuracy in the vernacular in the day-to-day life of Harlem. . . . His scale was big, but it was domestic, to be assimilated. . . . He never subscribed to the usual judgments of the vogue. In his time he imposed fashion."

Van Vechten's critical writings, whether on dance, the theatre, music and opera, or the more personal essays that were often autobiographical, were individual and candid. They were filled with grace and elegant phrasing, containing a mixture of youthful enthusiasm and worldly sophistication that expressed exactly what was on his mind. In an article called "Pastiches et Pistaches," in *The Reviewer* for July 1922, he wrote of the critic's place in the scheme of things: "The only thing a critic has it in his power to destroy is himself." This same criterion can be applied to the best of his photography. It is personal, highly subjective, and based on long experience in the arts. In his most extensive essay on his work as a photographer, which appeared in *Esquire* (December 1962), he called photography the most exigent of mistresses, both demanding and rewarding. He thought of it as the most fascinating of the arts.

In his personal correspondence in the late years Van Vechten candidly expressed his critical opinions, and the immediacy of his comments still hits hard. Formal writing for publication would not have allowed him such liberties. The following quotes are from letters written to his biographer, Bruce Kellner, between 1951 and 1964, on the subject of dance and dancers:

"I don't think the Sadler's Wells will be very good. It is the SCHOOL Ballet and the *big* ballet doesn't interest me much, aside from *Sleeping Beauty*, which is terrific. . . . You must remember when you differ from me about the ballet (or anything else) that often you have seen something only once, or only one company, while these old eyes have seen dozens of ballets, dozens of times . . . in *Coppélia* I have seen Pavlova, Danilova, and especially Slavenska. It is a ballet for a virtuosa and I would not be interested in seeing it done by pupils of a school. I guess it is for the same reason I don't like *The River* [a Renoir film of the period]. I have seen so much more beautiful Hindu dancing, and myself take pictures in so much better color, that it bores me, especially the story, and that silly boy with a neurosis. . . ."

(Regarding Sadler's Wells) "Assuredly the company has style, they furnish a pleasing spectacle, but no won-

John Martin, 1956

Lincoln Kirstein, 1933

Lincoln Kirstein, 1964

derful moments in the dancing, no acting, at all. No personalities. . . . And last night [1953] I saw *The Sleeping Beauty* and Sadler's Wells is back in favor again. It is such a beautiful production and by far the best thing SW does. Nadia Nerina danced Aurora and she is as refreshing as a bubbling spring. Oliver Messel's production is incredibly beautiful. Brian Shaw has wonderful elevation and Philip Chatfield was quite extraordinary too. . . ."

"I at last have Sadler's Wells placed in my mind. It is a *spectacle* company rather than a ballet company and *Sylvia* [1952] is the greatest spectacle of the lot. . . . I have decided after years of trial and testing why I dislike Sadler's Wells and have thrown the whole job out of my life forever. Thus making for simplification. I have long had the feeling that every time I saw one of their new ballets, it was something I had seen before . . . this came about because these dancers are a crashing bore, they all dance alike and have no atmosphere (whatever costumes they assume they remain essentially middle class British), excitement, or any other pleasure giving qualities. They are DULL, DULL, DULL. . . ."

"Opinions differ about the Danish Ballet. You have to see it at least twice to get the hang of it. It differs entirely from our ballets. And it takes a little time to get used to its quiet charm, but Henning Kronstam is sensational. . . . *La Sylphide* is marvelous and the *Coppélia* about the best I have experienced. . . ."

"Without doubt you are very wrong about [Lupe] Serrano in *The Combat.* I saw her in this the other night and she gave the worst performance of that ballet I have ever seen, even worse than Colette Marchand whom I saw in Paris. . . . Her technique is strong and she gave a flawless technical performance, but one utterly without feeling. To compare her with Melissa Hayden, who has so much feeling in the role, is sacrilege of the first order. . . . The critics have finally decided that Nora Kaye is NO *Giselle* and said so in no uncertain terms. I said so when I originally saw her. Margot Fonteyn is no *Giselle* either, I might add. . . . She actually has dancing faults. In *Giselle* she is almost ridiculous. She always stays too close to earth and is actually heavy and commonplace at times. She has one great part: Aurora in *The Sleeping Beauty.* No one can quite touch her in that. . . ."

(Concerning Ashton's *Ondine*) "Brian Shaw and Alexander Grant do whatever dancing is done, in an extremely English pantomime style, and it struck me during the proceedings that that is exactly what these ballet-spectacles are, a revival of the good old English pantomime. . . ."

"At long last I saw the Russians [Moiseyev] yesterday [1958], but aside from there being more of them, better disciplined in the staging, a fine band, and an excellently arranged program there is little, save two magnificent numbers that sets it apart from other folk dancers, such as the Yugoslavs, the Jews from Israel, the most original of all, or the Spaniards. In fact, I find Spanish gypsies in-

finitely more exciting and even American Indian war dances seen in full regalia and trappings are much more exciting. The two dances that raised my greatest interest were the dance in which the men entered (presumably) on horseback and raced around the stage which ended the first part and The Fight in the second part. Also when you have an indefinite number of Russians leaping to great heights with the women in their sexy variations you will know where Fokine got the idea for *Prince Igor.* Also, I once saw and heard the Hungarian cavalry playing the Rackosky March on coronets on galloping horses. You couldn't beat that."

In a 1943 letter to painter-sculptor George George, Van Vechten voiced his opinions on several of the male dancers of the day, which are intriguing from our vantage point of almost forty years later: "No male dancer in my experience has come anywhere near to the greatness of Nijinsky. As a poetic figure, Hugh Laing brings some of Nijinsky back, but Laing's technique is far from finished. Dolin is a good showman. [Frederic] Franklin has vigor, but no vitality. When he stands still he is not visible. I saw Massine make his first appearance in an important part in *The Legend of Joseph* [London, 1913]. I did not admire him then and I have seldom found any pleasure in watching him perform since. I like him somewhat more as a choreographer."

Van Vechten was fortunate in being in the right place at the right time in the first decades of this century; he observed the dance at its most rebellious and innovative. He would have agreed with Arlene Croce when she recently said that "classical style is mutable from generation to generation." In his letter to Kellner he said he had not seen *a* ballet or *a* performer in a role, but scores of productions and numberless dancers in the roles—all giving individual interpretations. Mature judgment, he said, is the result of continuing exposure to the repertoire; this is as important to the critic as is constant practice to the dancer. The century's early choreographers and dancers employed an originality—the single most important factor—in the interpretations of their work, making it the most exciting period in the history of dance. The surge of originality seemed to have leveled off by mid-century. Happily, some of the great artists from the first half of the century are still creating new works; it is a hard act for the less experienced to follow. It is not enough to be merely "in the style of."

Van Vechten in his eighties was a flamboyant character, instantly recognizable in New York theatre lobbies. At the dedication ceremony for the Martha Graham dance studio at the New School for Social Research, Van Vechten was one of the invited guests. Jane Kramer of the *Village Voice* (September 27, 1962) described him as he appeared that day: "The dance critics slipped in un-noticed, John Martin, for thirty years the dance writer for the *New York Times,* and Carl Van Vechten, the critic who preceded him. No sooner had he hobbled in than

Van Vechten, ageless and slightly terrifying in a turquoise button-down and a royal blue tie, his sparse hair combed into bangs, was dragged back into the corridor again by the photographers. They all took turns shooting at Van Vechten, who over the years had come to resemble a kindly werewolf and was therefore a perfect subject. . . ."

It was about this time in Van Vechten's life that I knew him. Although Carl lived in New York and I was in San Francisco, we corresponded regularly between my frequent visits to New York. The following excerpts from a few of his letters to me show him as he was at the end of his life: physically frail, but intellectually full of life and the master of every situation:

"I am not likely to meet you in San Francisco, because my travel days seem to be over. I used to travel extensively, before travelling became so difficult. My latest adventure was in 1949 when I visited London, Paris, and Rome. . . . I have been writing a little, a piece about Alvin Ailey for *Dance Perspectives*, for instance, and a tribute to Isak Dinesen, which will be published in a book of tributes coming out in December in Copenhagen, but I photograph all the time and that is my major interest now. Perhaps I told you that *Esquire* for December [1962] will carry my first article on photography as well as many photographs."

(After the *Esquire* article appeared) "My photographs were very badly reproduced in *Esquire*, and they were cropped, after they had promised they would not be. Of course, printing photographs on gray paper is almost enough to ruin them. . . . I never seem to have spare time. Photography takes a great deal of time. So does writing. Going to concerts, the opera and the theatre all take time. I scarcely have a moment to open a book. Christmas is nearly here and Christmas is a maelstrom in New York and probably in San Francisco too."

(November 1963) "The New York City Ballet opened its season on Tuesday very brilliantly indeed. Dick Banks, who is giving a portrait show of dancers in the hall off the auditorium invited eight people to go with him, and my wife and I were two of the guests. We had dinner and champagne at his house and sat in the front row. I like part of his picture show very much, but a good deal of it I don't like at all. He has talent but he is trying to do too much too quickly."

(May 15, 1963) "Today I am being photographed for *Esquire* in a group of authors from the Twenties and Thirties. I don't know who they can be. So few are living of this era. . . ." He wrote me a second letter later the same day: "I was photographed today with all the old timers still extant, for a double page in *Esquire* for July, which will appear two days before my birthday, on June 15. My photographees were Virgil Thomson, Malcolm Cowley, Dawn Powell, Marcel Duchamp, Man Ray, Glenway Wescott, Kay Boyle, Caresse Crosby, Matthew Josephson, William Slater Brown. Perhaps you had better get a Who's Who." When I inquired in my next letter who some of these persons were, he replied, "Hereafter, as here, I will use names indiscriminately without trying to identify them. You will eventually catch on."

When I was in New York in the spring of 1963, Carl sent a note to my hotel: "If you have nothing to do Saturday night, May 18, will you dine with me and go to hear Mabel Mercer at the club where she sings? She is marvellous and an old friend. I met her first thirty years ago in Paris shortly after you were born! . . . Banks is *bringing* the portrait of Gertrude Stein. . . . So we can all see it and I will photograph it." That evening Mabel Mercer was wearing a beautiful brocade gown made of Chinese silk that she told me she had bought in San Francisco, designed, and made herself. Carl photographed her in it a few days later.

(Fall 1963) "Markova sent us tickets for the dress rehearsal of the new production of *Aida* which opens the season. The scenic production is beautiful, but Birgit Nilsson is not my idea of Aida. However, Katherine Dunham has done a fine job with the choreography, danced largely by Negroes. On Tuesday we go to the rehearsal of *Manon* for which Markova has done the choreography."

"I saw the Great Martha Graham twice [in one week]. . . . Her *Judith* is by far the greatest performance the company gives. . . ."

"I am reading Max Beerbohm's Letters to Reggie Turner. I never met Beerbohm but I knew Turner well and photographed him when I was last in Florence, where he lived. That was a wonderful week I spent with Reggie, Norman Douglas, and Willie Maugham. . . ."

"You were a good boy and a good guest. You exhibited enthusiasm at the proper times and never seemed to be bored. It gave me a great pleasure to have you here. . . ."

THE DANCE
PHOTOGRAPHY
OF
CARL VAN VECHTEN

Charles Weidman in *School for Husbands*, 1933

Charles Weidman in *School for Husbands*, 1933

Charles Weidman, 1933

George Antheil, ballet composer, 1934

George M. Cohan, 1933

Orchidée (Lucille Hoff), who danced with Loie Fuller, 1933

William Dollar, 1935

Gypsy dancers, Granada, Spain, 1935

Vicente Escudero, 1933

Jose Fernandez, Mexican choreographer and dancer, 1939

Ram Gopal, 1938

Wilbur McCormick in his "Boxing" dance from *Olympiad*,
the Ted Shawn Dancers, 1938

Argentinita, 1940

Argentinita, 1940

Belle Rosette, 1941

Carmen Vazquez and Miguel Herrero in the Spanish revue,
Cabalgata, 1949

Eugene Von Grona, founder of American Negro Ballet, 1938

Leni Bouvier and Eugene Von Grona, 1938

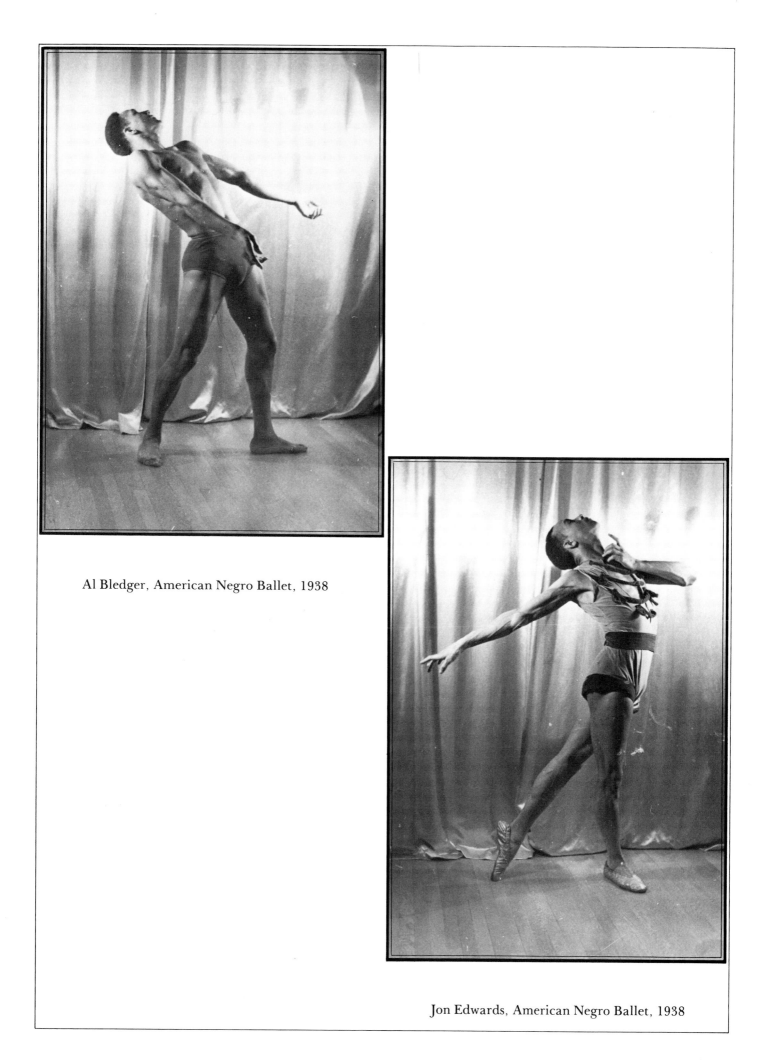

Al Bledger, American Negro Ballet, 1938

Jon Edwards, American Negro Ballet, 1938

Bill "Bojangles" Robinson, 1933

Bill "Bojangles" Robinson, 1933

Bill "Bojangles" Robinson, 1941

Cab Calloway, from Harlem's Cotton Club, 1933

Cab Calloway, from Harlem's Cotton Club, 1933

Roy Atkins, Cotton Club dancer, 1934

Louis Cole, Cotton Club dancer in Paris, 1934

Kaloah, exotic dancer in *Cotton Club Parade* on Broadway, 1936

Kaloah, exotic dancer in *Cotton Club Parade* on Broadway, 1936

John W. Bubbles, 1935

John W. Bubbles as Sportin' Life in Gershwin's *Porgy and Bess*, 1935

Avon Long as Sportin' Life in revival of *Porgy and Bess*, 1942

Asadata Dafora (Horton) in *Kykunkor*, 1935

Black Ritual, choreographed by Agnes de Mille for Ballet Theatre with an all-Negro cast, 1940. Maudelle Bass, Dorothy Williams, Muriel Cook

Lawayne Kennard and Maudelle Bass

Lawayne Kennard and Dorothy Williams

Katherine Dunham, 1940

Katherine Dunham, 1940

Archie Savage, Dunham Dancers, 1942

Eartha Kitt, Dunham Dancers, 1952

Claude Marchant, Dunham Dancers, 1947

Pearl Primus, 1943

Pearl Primus dancing *The Blues*, 1943

Janet Collins, 1949

Janet Collins dancing *Nobody Knows*, 1949

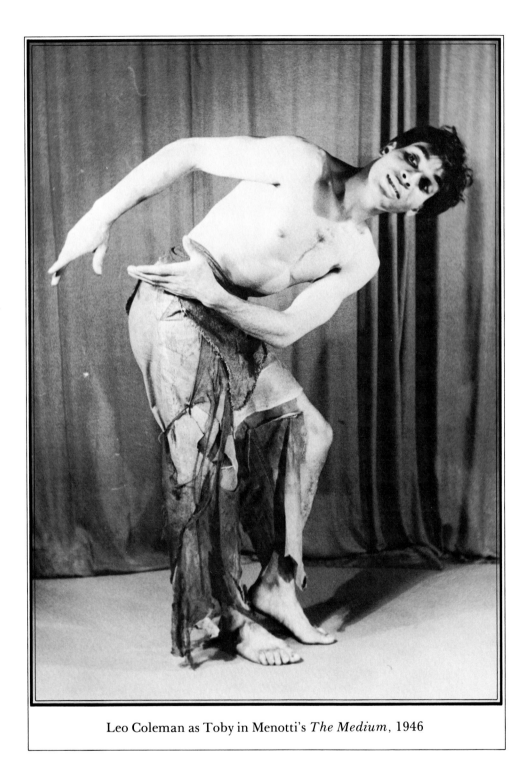

Leo Coleman as Toby in Menotti's *The Medium*, 1946

Gilda Gray, inventor of the "shimmy," 1940

Harrison Thomson as the Prince in *Sleeping Beauty* on ice, 1947

Harrison Thomson in *Howdy, Mr. Ice*, 1948

Rudy Richards in *Howdy, Mr. Ice*, 1948

Antony Tudor, 1940

Antony Tudor in *Gala Performance*, 1941

Hugh Laing, 1940

Hugh Laing in *Goya Pastorale*, 1940

Antony Tudor and Hugh Laing, 1940

Hugh Laing and Diana Adams, 1948

Hugh Laing, 1940

Hugh Laing in Java costume, 1940

Hugh Laing, 1940

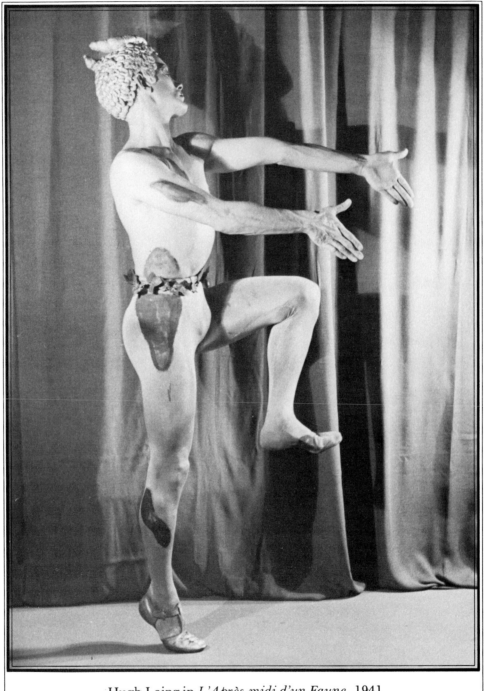

Hugh Laing in *L'Après-midi d'un Faune*, 1941

Hugh Laing and Sono Osato in *Pillar of Fire*, 1942

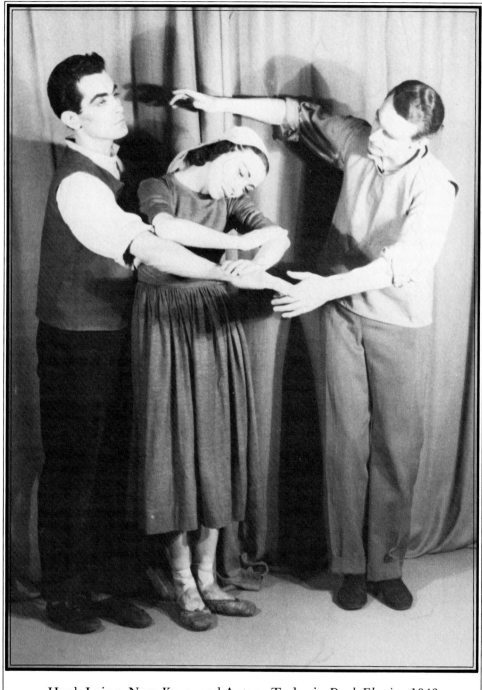

Hugh Laing, Nora Kaye, and Antony Tudor in *Dark Elegies*, 1943

Antony Tudor in *Jardin aux Lilas*, 1941

Hugh Laing in *Jardin aux Lilas*, 1941

Hugh Laing, Nora Kaye, Antony Tudor, and Annabelle Lyon in
Jardin aux Lilas, at Langnerlane Farm, 1941

Agnes de Mille, 1940

Agnes de Mille in *Judgment of Paris*, 1940

Agnes de Mille in *Judgment of Paris*, 1940

Antony Tudor, Hugh Laing, and Maria Karnilova in revival of
Judgment of Paris, 1943

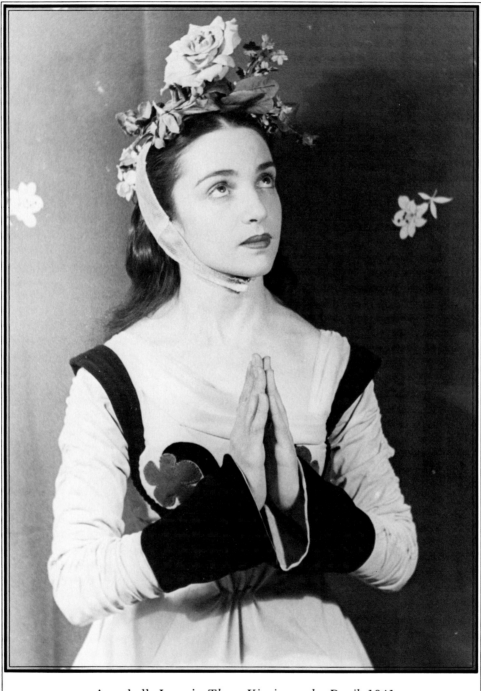

Annabelle Lyon in *Three Virgins and a Devil*, 1941

Lucia Chase in *Three Virgins and a Devil*, 1941

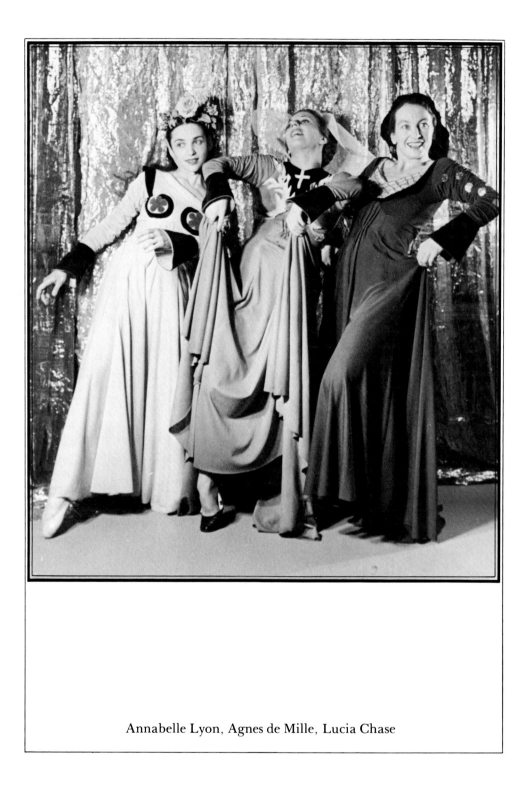

Annabelle Lyon, Agnes de Mille, Lucia Chase

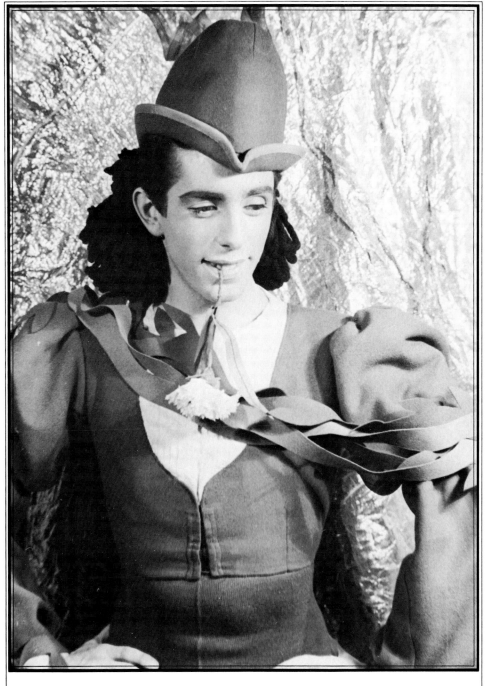

Jerome Robbins in *Three Virgins and a Devil*, 1941

Jerome Robbins in *Three Virgins and a Devil*, 1941

Alicia Markova, 1940

Alicia Markova in *Foyer de Danse* costume, 1940

Alicia Markova in *Bluebeard*, 1940

Anton Dolin and Alicia Markova in *Princess Aurora*, 1943

Alicia Markova in *Giselle*, Act One, 1941

Alicia Markova with lamb, 1944

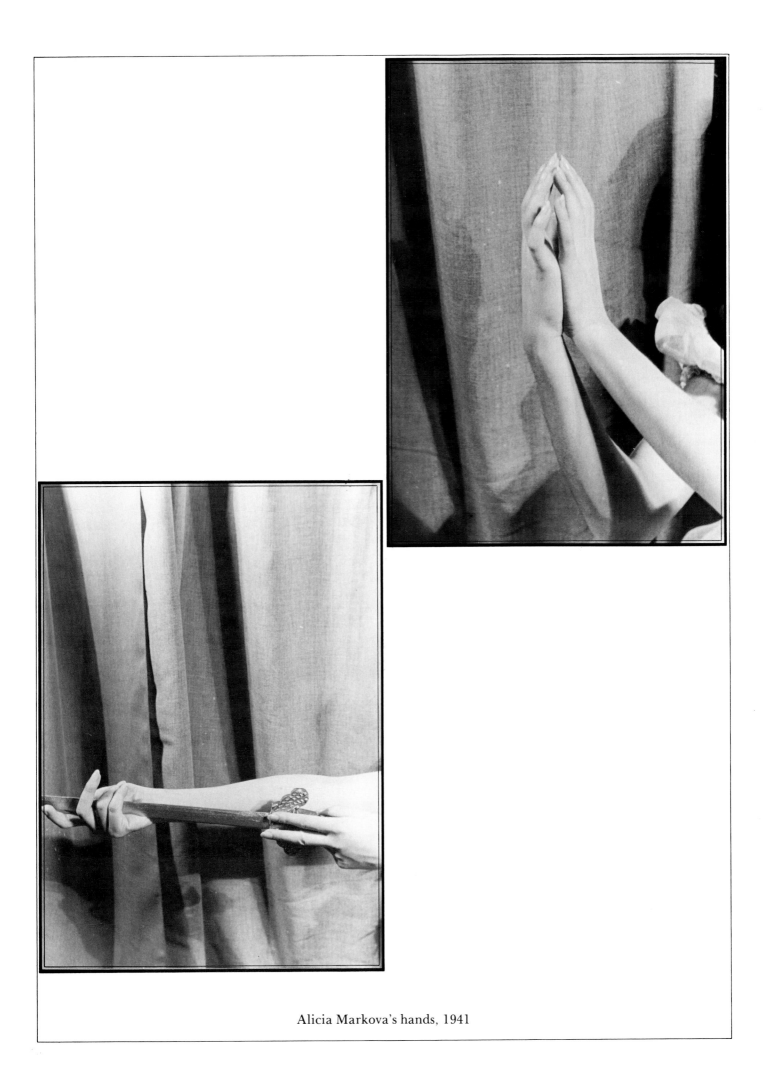

Alicia Markova's hands, 1941

Hugh Laing in *Aleko*, 1942

Hugh Laing and Alicia Markova in *Aleko*, 1942

Hugh Laing as Romeo, 1943

Hugh Laing and Alicia Markova in *Romeo and Juliet*, 1943

Alicia Markova as Camille, 1946

Alicia Markova as Camille, 1946

Alicia Markova as the "Dying Swan," 1948

Alicia Markova as the "Dying Swan," 1948

Alicia Markova, 1952

Alicia Markova in *Orfeo ed Euridice*, 1955

Oleg Briansky and Alicia Markova in *The Merry Widow*, 1955

Alicia Markova, 1963

Anton Dolin in a Spanish dance, 1940

Anton Dolin in *Swan Lake*, 1941

Ian Gibson in *Princess Aurora*, 1941

Annabelle Lyon in *Aurora's Wedding*, 1941

Nora Kaye and Hugh Laing in *Pillar of Fire*, 1942

Nora Kaye and Hugh Laing in *Petrouchka*, 1948

Nora Kaye in *Dim Lustre*, 1944

Hugh Laing and Nora Kaye in *Dim Lustre*, 1944

Nora Kaye in *Facsimile*, 1946

Nora Kaye in *Fall River Legend*, 1948

Jared French, set and costume designer, 1935

Lee Simonson, set designer, 1933

Irene Sharaff, set and costume designer, 1940

Marc Chagall, artist, set and costume designer, 1941

Donald Saddler, 1941

Donald Saddler as Alias in *Billy the Kid*, 1941

Janet Reed, 1944

Janet Reed and Hugh Laing in *Tally-Ho*, 1944

John Kriza in *Fancy Free*, 1949

John Kriza as *Billy the Kid*, 1949

Marcel Vertes, painter and designer, 1950

Oliver Smith, codirector of Ballet Theatre and designer, 1947

Virgil Thomson, composer, 1947

Aaron Copland, composer, 1935

Leonard Bernstein, composer, 1944

Michael Maule, 1954

Michael Maule as the Rich Boy in *Filling Station*, 1954

Diana Adams in *Shadow of the Wind*, 1948

Muriel Bentley in *Shadow of the Wind*, 1948

Hugh Laing in *Shadow of the Wind*, 1948

Eric Braun in *Shadow of the Wind*, 1948

Nana Gollner in *Shadow of the Wind*, 1948

André Eglevsky in *Prince Goudal's Festival*, 1944

André Eglevsky in *Prince Goudal's Festival*, 1944

Todd Bolender in *The Four Temperaments*, 1947

Todd Bolender in *The Four Temperaments*, 1947

Francisco Moncion as *Sebastian*, 1944

Viola Essen as the Courtesan in *Sebastian*, 1944

Nathalie Krassovska as Grahn in *Pas de Quatre*, 1948

Alicia Markova, Nathalie Krassovska, and Alexandra Danilova in
Pas de Quatre, 1948

Mia Slavenska as Grisi in *Pas de Quatre*, 1948

Alicia Markova as Taglioni in *Pas de Quatre*, 1948

Mia Slavenska, Alexandra Danilova, Alicia Markova, and
Nathalie Krassovska in *Pas de Quatre*, 1948

Alexandra Danilova as Cerito in *Pas de Quatre*, 1948

Milorad Miskovitch in *L'Après-midi d'un Faune*, 1954

Milorad Miskovitch in *L'Après-midi d'un Faune*, 1954

Milorad Miskovitch and Alicia Markova in *L'Après-midi d'un Faune*, 1954

Josephine Baker at *Folies Bergère*, Paris, 1949

Josephine Baker, backstage at Strand Theatre, New York, 1951

James Mitchell in *Paint Your Wagon*, 1952

Mary Burr in *Paint Your Wagon*, 1952

Tamara Chapman and Dorothy Hill in *Paint Your Wagon*, 1952

Ni-Gusti-Raka, nine-year-old Balinese dancer, 1952

Iris Mabry, 1954

Melissa Hayden, 1956

Violette Verdy in Balanchine's *Serenade*, 1961

Alvin Ailey, 1955

Alvin Ailey, 1955

Alvin Ailey, 1955

Carmen de Lavallade, 1955

Carmen de Lavallade and Geoffrey Holder, 1955

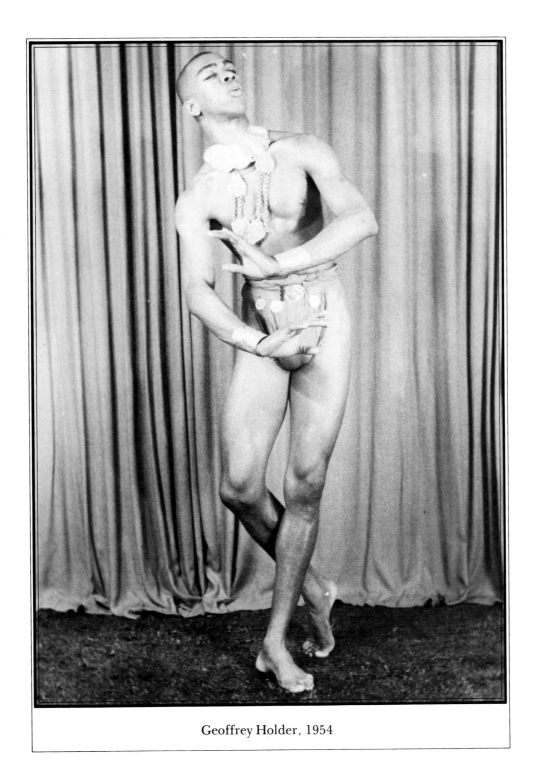

Geoffrey Holder, 1954

Geoffrey Holder, Scoogie Brown, and Alphonso Marshall, 1954

Charles Blackwell in Watusi costume, 1955

Arthur Mitchell, 1955

Arthur Mitchell, 1955

Bill Earl in *The Figure in the Carpet*, 1961

Hernán Baldrich, Chilean dancer, in *At the Beach*, 1962

Paul Taylor, 1960

Paul Taylor in Balanchine's *Episodes*, 1960

Paul Taylor in *The Least Flycatcher*, 1960

Isamu Noguchi, sculptor and set designer, 1935

Isamu Noguchi, sculptor and set designer, 1935

Jean Rosenthal, lighting and production designer, 1951

Martha Graham and Bertram Ross in *Visionary Recital*, 1961

Martha Graham and Bertram Ross in *Visionary Recital*, 1961

Martha Graham and Bertram Ross in *Clytemnestra*, 1961

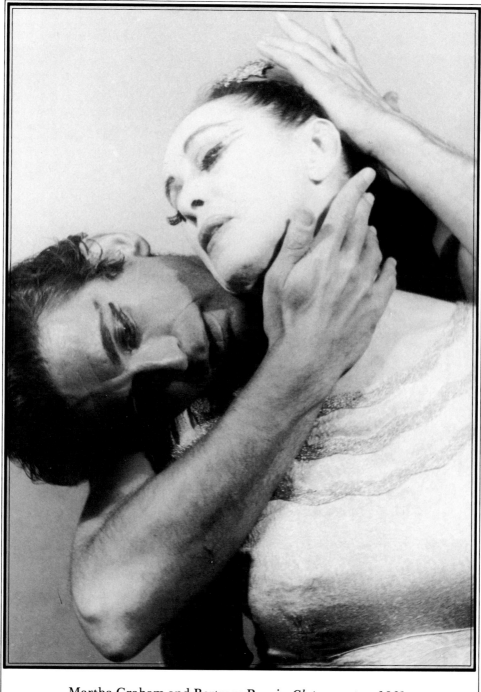

Martha Graham and Bertram Ross in *Clytemnestra*, 1961

Martha Graham and Bertram Ross in *Clytemnestra,* 1961

INDEX